NATALIE COLE · ELIZABETH COTTEN · ELLA FITZGERALD · ROBERTA FLA
DYS KNIGHT · PATTI LABELLE · ABBEY LINCOLN · DARLENE LOVE · BARBA
RTON · DIANA ROSS · JILL SCOTT · NINA SIMONE · SISTER NANCY · SKIN
AH VAUGHAN · DIONNE WARWICK · DINAH WASHINGTON · NANCY WILSON · SADE ADU · ERYKAH BADU ·
OTTEN · ELLA FITZGERALD · ROBERTA FLACK · ARETHA FRANKLIN · BILLIE HOLIDAY · LENA HORNE · JANET
ABBEY LINCOLN · DARLENE LOVE · BARBARA LYNN · RITA MARLEY · MC LYTE · MEMPHIS MINNIE · ODETTA
SCOTT · NINA SIMONE · SISTER NANCY · SKIN · BESSIE SMITH · RONNIE SPECTOR · MAVIS STAPLES · POLY
WARWICK · DINAH WASHINGTON · NANCY WILSON · SADE ADU · ERYKAH BADU · ANITA BAKER · BEYONCÉ
ALD · ROBERTA FLACK · ARETHA FRANKLIN · BILLIE HOLIDAY · LENA HORNE · JANET JACKSON · MAHALIA
LENE LOVE · BARBARA LYNN · RITA MARLEY · MC LYTE · MEMPHIS MINNIE · ODETTA · THE POINTER SISTERS
STER NANCY · SKIN · BESSIE SMITH · RONNIE SPECTOR · MAVIS STAPLES · POLY STYRENE · SISTER ROSETTA
GTON · NANCY WILSON · SADE ADU · ERYKAH BADU · ANITA BAKER · BEYONCÉ · DEE DEE BRIDGEWATER
RETHA FRANKLIN · BILLIE HOLIDAY · LENA HORNE · JANET JACKSON · MAHALIA JACKSON · ETTA JAMES
LYNN · RITA MARLEY · MC LYTE · MEMPHIS MINNIE · ODETTA · THE POINTER SISTERS · LEONTYNE PRICE
BESSIE SMITH · RONNIE SPECTOR · MAVIS STAPLES · POLY STYRENE · SISTER ROSETTA THARPE · BIG MAMA
SADE ADU · ERYKAH BADU · ANITA BAKER · BEYONCÉ · DEE DEE BRIDGEWATER · BETTY CARTER · TRACY
HOLIDAY · LENA HORNE · JANET JACKSON · MAHALIA JACKSON · ETTA JAMES · CHAKA KHAN · ANGÉLIQUE
TE · MEMPHIS MINNIE · ODETTA · THE POINTER SISTERS · LEONTYNE PRICE · QUEEN LATIFAH · MA RAINEY
CTOR · MAVIS STAPLES · POLY STYRENE · SISTER ROSETTA THARPE · BIG MAMA THORNTON · TINA TURNER
U · ANITA BAKER · BEYONCÉ · DEE DEE BRIDGEWATER · BETTY CARTER · TRACY CHAPMAN · NATALIE COLE
ANET JACKSON · MAHALIA JACKSON · ETTA JAMES · CHAKA KHAN · ANGÉLIQUE KIDJO · GLADYS KNIGHT
ETTA · THE POINTER SISTERS · LEONTYNE PRICE · QUEEN LATIFAH · MA RAINEY · MINNIE RIPERTON · DIANA
Y STYRENE · SISTER ROSETTA THARPE · BIG MAMA THORNTON · TINA TURNER · ARI UP · SARAH VAUGHAN
DEE DEE BRIDGEWATER · BETTY CARTER · TRACY CHAPMAN · NATALIE COLE · ELIZABETH COTTEN · ELLA
KSON · ETTA JAMES · CHAKA KHAN · ANGÉLIQUE KIDJO · GLADYS KNIGHT · PATTI LABELLE · ABBEY LINCOLN
LEONTYNE PRICE · QUEEN LATIFAH · MA RAINEY · MINNIE RIPERTON · DIANA ROSS · JILL SCOTT · NINA
A THARPE · BIG MAMA THORNTON · TINA TURNER · ARI UP · SARAH VAUGHAN · DIONNE WARWICK · DINAH
TTY CARTER · TRACY CHAPMAN · NATALIE COLE · ELIZABETH COTTEN · ELLA FITZGERALD · ROBERTA FLACK
HAN · ANGÉLIQUE KIDJO · GLADYS KNIGHT · PATTI LABELLE · ABBEY LINCOLN · DARLENE LOVE · BARBARA
IFAH · MA RAINEY · MINNIE RIPERTON · DIANA ROSS · JILL SCOTT · NINA SIMONE · SISTER NANCY · SKIN
N · TINA TURNER · ARI UP · SARAH VAUGHAN · DIONNE WARWICK · DINAH WASHINGTON · NANCY WILSON

SHE RAISED HER VOICE!

SHE RAISED HER VOICE!

50 BLACK WOMEN
WHO SANG THEIR WAY INTO
MUSIC HISTORY

Written by
JORDANNAH ELIZABETH

Illustrated by
BRIANA DENGOUE

RP KIDS
PHILADELPHIA

Running Press Kids
Hachette Book Group
1290 Avenue of the Americas, New York, NY 10104
www.runningpress.com/rpkids
@RP_Kids

Printed in China

First Edition: December 2021

Published by Running Press Kids, an imprint of Perseus Books, LLC, a subsidiary of Hachette Book Group, Inc. The Running Press Kids name and logo is a trademark of the Hachette Book Group.

The Hachette Speakers Bureau provides a wide range of authors for speaking events. To find out more, go to www.hachettespeakersbureau.com or call (866) 376-6591.

The publisher is not responsible for websites (or their content) that are not owned by the publisher.

Print book cover and interior design by Frances J. Soo Ping Chow.
Interior and cover illustrations by Briana Dengoue

Library of Congress Cataloging-in-Publication Data
Names: Elizabeth, Jordannah, author. | Dengoue, Briana, illustrator.
Title: She raised her voice : 50 black women who sang their way into music history /
written by Jordannah Elizabeth; illustrated by Briana Dengoue.
Description: First edition. | Philadelphia : Running Press Kids, 2021. | Includes index. |
Audience: Ages 8-12 | Audience: Grades 4-6
Identifiers: LCCN 2021000662 (print) | LCCN 2021000663 (ebook) | ISBN 9780762475162 (hardcover) |
ISBN 9780762475155 (ebook) | ISBN 9780762475148 (ebook)
Subjects: LCSH: African American women singers—Biography—Juvenile literature. | African American singers—
Biography—Juvenile literature. | Women singers—United States—Biography—Juvenile literature.
Classification: LCC ML3929 .E55 2021 (print) | LCC ML3929 (ebook) | DDC 782.42164092/2 [B]—dc23
LC record available at https://lccn.loc.gov/2021000662
LC ebook record available at https://lccn.loc.gov/2021000663

ISBNs: 978-0-7624-7516-2 (hardcover), 978-0-7624-7514-8 (ebook)

1010

10 9 8 7 6 5 4 3 2 1

For all the girls whose dreams seem impossible. I promise you, nothing is impossible!

—J. E.

CONTENTS

Introduction . . . viii

INTRODUCTION

When I was a young girl, the things that brought me joy and peace were reading and listening to music. I especially remember the first time I heard Nina Simone sing. A warm feeling washed over me and just by the simple act of listening to her voice, I felt like my life had changed. I was hearing a voice that effected change in the world. As the years went by, I felt the same way about hearing other Black women singers, like Betty Carter, Sade Adu, Sarah Vaughan, and Abbey Lincoln.

By listening to these women, I learned a lot about myself: what I liked and what I didn't. I learned about what love can feel like and how to live bravely even during heartache.

There was a time when Black women were expected to do nothing more than clean houses and care for children. We were denied education, voting rights, and a warm night's sleep in a hotel or a seat on a bus or access to an ordinary restaurant. The world seemed to tell us that we weren't valued or loved.

The women in this book carried on through the harshness of the world by stepping onto stages, many times as glamorous goddesses, wearing beautiful dresses and glittery diamonds, but sometimes simply in T-shirts and jeans or leather pants, to show us that Black women have talent, grace, and the right to entertain whoever is willing to hear us.

Not only did the women included in this book spread the message of equality just by having the courage to sing in front of large crowds, but they also often sang about social change, feminism, civil rights, and their personal need for love. They marched in protests and sang gospel and spirituals of the Black church to uplift people when everything in the world seemed to be going wrong.

These women overcame fear and sadness so they could give us—the music fans—the gifts that they were born with and worked hard to perfect.

I wrote about the musical history of these women so that you can discover the great joy they have brought to *my* life along with the lives of millions of other music lovers. I find it to be my duty and honor to share how special and successful these women became by believing in themselves and giving their lives fully to music.

Once you read the stories in this book, do your best to listen to the music these women made and continue to make. Get to know their voices and sing along with them. Their music will fill your heart with happiness and heal you when you are in pain. They'll show you cool tricks you can do with your voice, and they may even inspire you to make music yourself!

Find freedom in this book, because I truly believe that's what every woman included within these pages wanted or currently wants for you—the freedom to choose and the freedom to express yourself without fear that people won't love you if you are your true self.

As a kid, you have a whole wide world to explore, and reading about these women can help you find out more about who you could grow up to be. Even if you don't want to be a singer or musician, you can learn from these women about how to change the world—how to give back when you're given a lot, how to believe in yourself when times get hard, and how being yourself is the best thing you can possibly be. Life gives you gifts when you learn and grow. These amazing women raised their voices and sang from their hearts. How will you raise your voice? How will you show the world what's truly in your mind and heart? This book can reveal the seeds of who you're going to become.

Sade Adu

(B. JANUARY 16, 1959)

R&B / SOUL

The Queen of Subtle Soul

"Once a song's out there, it's no longer mine. And that's the whole purpose of music: to belong to people."

—SADE ADU

Unlike many lead singers, Sade Adu (pronounced *shaw-day*) is not in love with the spotlight and the attention (and sometimes trouble) that fame brings to an artist's world. She holds her life, friends, and family close to her heart, shielding them from spying photographers, curious journalists, and the millions of fans she has received just by being herself.

Born Helen Folasade Adu in the African country of Nigeria, Sade moved with her mother to England when she was four years old. She didn't study music as a child but rather went to school to study fashion design when she was seventeen. After finishing school, she worked as a model for a few years, and it wasn't until 1980, when Sade was twenty-one, that she decided to take a chance on making music.

Sade was offered a job as a backup singer for a British band called Pride. While working with Sade, the band's saxophonist, Stuart Matthewman, realized she was a good

songwriter, and the two began writing songs together. They worked hard as a team and started playing their songs during Pride shows. Word about the band began to spread, and record label executives started to take notice of Sade's calm and sullen voice, especially on a song called "Smooth Operator."

Realizing that they had a special musical bond, both musicians left Pride to start their own group—called Sade—with drummer Paul Cooke, bass player Paul Denman, and keyboardist Andrew Hale. The newly formed group played to a sold-out nightclub on their first show! It is said that one thousand people weren't able to even get into the club because there was no room to hold them. Many musicians play for only a small group of people when they first begin to tour, but Sade's music was hypnotic, like drawing moths to a lightbulb.

Sade and her band signed a record deal and released their first album, *Diamond Life*, in 1984. This album sold more than six million copies across many countries, making Sade's debut the best-selling album by a woman singer in British history—and the band's song "Smooth Operator" became a top-selling hit. The next year, Sade and her band released their second album, *Promise*, which was even more successful than their first. It became the band's first number-one-selling album and includes the song "The Sweetest Taboo," which is one of their most memorable to this day.

In 1986, Sade tried her hand at acting, playing Athene Duncannon in a film called *Absolute Beginners*. Her band's next two albums—*Stronger Than Pride* (1988) and *Love Deluxe* (1992)—went on to sell millions of copies, but as well as things were going, Sade didn't record another album for eight years following the birth of her son. Nonetheless, after so many years of her not recording music or playing shows, the world seemed to love Sade more and more.

The band returned with *Lovers Rock* (2000) and *Soldier of Love* (2010). Even though Sade has recorded only six albums in thirty years, her band is one of the most successful music groups on the planet. Sade has a deep connection with her fans that spans space and time, and they continue to love her even when she is silent.

Erykah Badu

(B. FEBRUARY 26, 1971)

NEO-SOUL

The First Lady of Neo-Soul

*"I grew up with all mothers, all women. I come from
a long line of matriarchs, very strong women."*

—ERYKAH BADU

Erica Abi Wright has a look that stands out among the many songstresses who came before and after her. Growing up, Erica's talent shown through at an early age. When she was four she enjoyed performing at Dallas Theater Center and the Black Academy of Arts and Letters (her uncle was its founder and her godmother watched over her). When she was fourteen years old she changed her name from Erica to Erykah to reflect her spiritual views of the world: "kah" means inner self and "badu" is her favorite jazz scat sound.

She graduated from Booker T. Washington High School for the Performing and Visual Arts and attended college, but as her love for music grew Erykah knew she had to pursue it full time. And in 1993, she left college to do just that. She worked several odd jobs and performed in a

group with her cousin Robert "Free" Bradford. The duo released a demo album called *Country Cousins*, which attracted music producer Kedar Massenburg. In 1995, Kedar connected Erykah with the chance to sing a duet with the up-and-coming R&B soul artist D'Angelo on the song "Your Precious Love," which was originally sung by Marvin Gaye and Tammy Terrell in 1967. Erykah showed that she was poised and ready to grow in her career and signed a record deal with Kedar Entertainment.

In 1996, before her catchy song "On & On" was released to eager listeners, Erykah wore large headwraps and bright colors that mirrored the style of African and Black women who lived in her neighborhood in Brooklyn, New York. Many say that she sang like Billie Holiday, but her music had a newer sound that merged hip-hop, blues, jazz, and soul. This caused some to label her music neo-soul (neo meaning "new"). Once Erykah's first full album, *Baduizm*, came out, she showed everyone that not only could she look different, but she could also create unique soundscapes of catchy, earthy songs that make you want to move and sing along.

Erykah's artful lyrics didn't just focus on topics of love and loss; she often sang about spirituality and Mother Earth. For example, her song "Next Lifetime" was about her being with her love in a different lifetime, which is based on the idea of reincarnation, the theory that people live many different lives over the course of time. This concept comes mostly from Asian religions like Hinduism and Buddhism. These concepts—and her expression of them through music—made Erykah a very wise musician along with being a beautiful singer.

Baduizm sold more than three million copies and opened the door for Erykah to have a twenty-year career, which is still going strong today. Her second album (released in 2000), *Mama's Gun*, was another hit and included her now-famous song "Bag Lady." The song is impactful, written about a woman who needs to let go of her life's problems that are weighing her down (as if she were carrying several heavy bags on her shoulders). Erykah went on to release more albums over the years, like *Worldwide Underground* and *New Amerykah Part One* and *Part Two*. She even wrote and reimagined a version of Drake's song "Hotline Bling" on her 2015 mixtape *But You Caint Use My Phone*.

Erykah is also widely known for her live performances. She is a popular DJ who loves to make crowds dance and have fun. Her earthy style and sweet, sensuous voice, along with her beautiful eccentricities, make Erykah one of the most favored and fun soul singers in music history.

Anita Baker

(B. JANUARY 26, 1958)

R&B

R&B Songstress /
Overcomer of Early Challenges

*"You leave home to seek your fortune and,
when you get it, you go home and share it
with your family."*

—ANITA BAKER

 nita Baker is an R&B star who took the world by storm with her romantic and sultry music, but her life wasn't necessarily a fairy tale of fame and adoration. Anita's father was not around when she was a baby, and when she turned two years old, her mother left. Because she didn't have any parents to care for her, she grew up in a foster family in Detroit, Michigan. If that wasn't difficult enough, Anita's foster parents passed away when she was twelve, and she was then raised by her foster sister until she was old enough to make it on her own.

Anita started to find her path in music when she was sixteen. She began to perform live in different places around Detroit. She was so determined and talented that she caught the attention of a musician named David Washington, who asked her to join his funk band, Chapter 8. She fit in well and the group was offered a record deal.

Things seemed to be looking up for Anita, but her road to stardom was still bumpy. Her band lost their record deal after recording their first album, and Anita was told that she didn't have enough talent to make it big as a solo singer. Saddened and discouraged, she went back to Detroit and began working as a receptionist and waitress.

A few years later, and seemingly out of nowhere, Anita received a lucky break when one of the people who worked at her old record label contacted her and convinced her to record her own music. She released her first solo album, *The Songstress*, in 1983, and it was a success!

Nonetheless, Anita still had to work hard and fight for her chance to touch the world. It's been said that she didn't receive some of the money that she earned from the sales of her first solo album and that her record label wasn't moving very fast on putting out her second album. She had to go to court to fight for her freedom to record her music with a different label.

But where there's struggle, there can also be a road to success. Anita's second album, *Rapture*, got the R&B singer her first pop hit with the song "Sweet Love" in 1986, and it went on to sell more than eight million copies and even won her two Grammy Awards!

Throughout her career, Anita has sold millions more records. She was even given an honorary doctorate of music from Berklee College of Music, proving that she was able to overcome adversity, all while being a very intelligent musical mind. Anita proves that it pays to never give up!

Beyoncé

(B. SEPTEMBER 4, 1981)

R&B / POP

Queen Bey

*"I felt like it was time
to set up my future, so I set a goal.
My goal was independence."*

—BEYONCÉ

Beyoncé Giselle Knowles-Carter has shown herself to be one of the most powerful postmodern Black woman pop stars in music history. She received her first taste of stardom when she won a talent show at seven years old by singing John Lennon's song "Imagine," beating out high school kids who were competing against her.

As she grew older she became part of one of the best-selling girl groups of all time: Destiny's Child. This amazing group of young women sang songs like "Independent Women Part I" and "Survivor" that empowered girls to be self-assured and strong within themselves. But in the beginning of the group's success, Beyoncé faced some troubles and deep depression, as members of the group were fired and changed out, causing her to experience backlash from her fans. She overcame the painful moments and her depression with the help of her mother, Tina Knowles-Lawson, and moved forward with the group and her career.

After five chart-topping albums between 1998 and 2004, Destiny's Child disbanded, and Beyoncé began focusing on building one of the world's most impressive solo music careers.

Beyoncé's solo career began a couple of years before Destiny's Child officially parted ways. She recorded a song with the man who would become her husband, Jay-Z, in 2002, as they teamed up on "03 Bonnie & Clyde." The song would appear on the international version of her first solo album, *Dangerously in Love*, in 2003. From this album, "Crazy in Love" emerged as her very first number-one song. She toured Europe and mesmerized her fans. In 2006, she formed an all-woman band called Suga Mama to sing backup vocals on her worldwide tour.

As Beyoncé became more famous, she realized that she needed an outlet that would separate her quieter, shy personality from the strong, aggressive, and highly confident woman she wanted to be onstage. Thus, Sasha Fierce—her alter ego—was born. Sasha is more outgoing and intense, giving Beyoncé more personal power to move her art forward. In 2008, she released *I Am . . . Sasha Fierce*. In 2012, she was honored with singing at President Barack Obama's inaugural ball to celebrate his being elected. She's acted in numerous films, including *Carmen: A Hip Hopera*, *Dreamgirls*, and the spy comedy *The Pink Panther*.

Her 2016 album, *Lemonade*, was released as a visual album that focused on issues of racism and relationships. This short film series opened the door for Beyoncé to create *Black Is King*, a full-length film that reimagined the story of *The Lion King* (she also starred in the live-action remake of the Disney film in 2019). Her style and her countless accomplishments make Beyoncé one of the hardest-working women musicians of all time. Her dedication to her belief in feminism and her work to create a better world for Black people and young girls make her a true icon in both the music industry and pop culture.

Dee Dee Bridgewater

(B. MAY 27, 1950)

JAZZ

A Bright Star in Music and on the Stage

"I was very adamant about not being called a jazz singer, but now I've embraced it. The way I approach music is through jazz, so I'm a jazz singer."

—DEE DEE BRIDGEWATER

D ee Dee Bridgewater (born Denise Garrett) learned about jazz from her father, who was a jazz trumpet player and schoolteacher. This early influence inspired her to join a jazz band while attending college, which allowed her to travel the world as a young woman in the late 1960s.

Soon after graduating, she met her husband, Cecil Bridgewater, who was a jazz trumpeter just like her father. The couple moved to New York City to pursue music. Dee Dee's career as a jazz musician took off when she was hired as the lead singer for the Thad Jones–Mel Lewis Jazz Orchestra in the early 1970s. Things continued to look up for her as she recorded her first

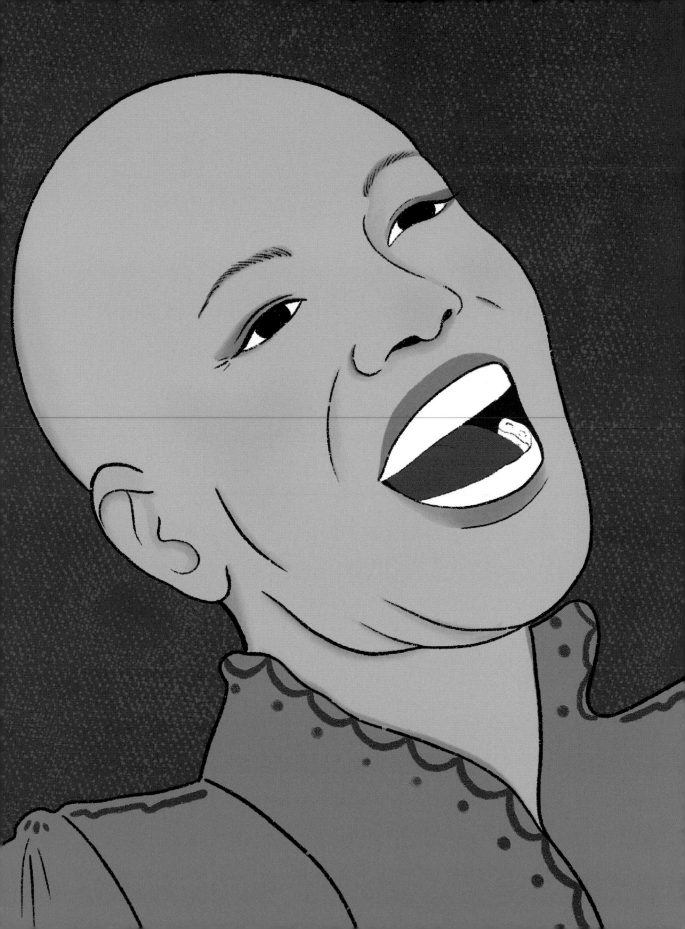

album, *Afro Blue*, in 1974, and landed a lead role in the famous reimagined *Wizard of Oz* musical *The Wiz*. She also played the beloved vocalist Billie Holiday in the musical *Lady Day*.

Not only is Dee Dee a wonderful singer in her own right, but she loves and respects the amazing jazz singers who came before her. She recorded an album paying tribute to Ella Fitzgerald called *Dear Ella* (1997) and an album showcasing her admiration for Billie Holiday called *Eleanora Fagan (1915–1959): To Billie with Love from Dee Dee* (2010). She is also very well-traveled and worldly. Dee Dee moved to Paris, France, and recorded an album in French called *J'ai Deux Amours* (2005); later, she recorded a record based on African music called *Red Earth* (2007).

Dee Dee loves—and is loved by—many cultures. Dee Dee's voice is unforgettable. It is smooth and romantic and makes you feel like you are sailing freely on the ocean on a perfect summer day. She has won many awards from around the globe for her singing and stage performances.

Outside of her music, Dee Dee helps the world as the United Nations Goodwill Ambassador for the Food and Agriculture Organization—just like singer Dionne Warwick! This means she works hard to make sure people all over the world have the food they need to be healthy and strong. Dee Dee has been able to use her popularity as a singer to positively and effectively help those who are less fortunate.

Betty Carter

(MAY 19, 1929, TO SEPTEMBER 26, 1998)

JAZZ

Unique and Out of the Box

"If you've got a heart at all, I'm going to get it."

—BETTY CARTER

Jazz singer Betty Carter is known to be one of the most inventive and musically courageous vocalists and jazz composers of her time. Betty got her start in the music business as a teenager in the 1940s by singing with jazz legends Charlie Parker and Dizzy Gillespie. In a time when big bands were the leaders of the jazz sound, and vocalists like Ella Fitzgerald, Billie Holiday, and Sarah Vaughan reigned as queens of jazz, Betty knew she had to stand out and define herself as a singer who explored new ways of using her vocals in the genre.

Betty's career took off when she was hired to sing for musician Lionel Hampton's orchestra. It has been widely proclaimed that Betty and Lionel didn't get along too well, but they did make great music together. Betty is said to be one of the last big band singers, and as such, she sang her way into the new era of jazz called "bebop," which was a more experimental and improvised kind of jazz. Betty was so good at scatting and improvising that she was nicknamed Betty Bebop (a name she didn't like very much). Nevertheless, this made her one of the earliest bebop singers in jazz history. Over the years, she crafted a singing style that was clear, smooth, and off-kilter, and she started a solo career in 1951, soon after she left Hampton's influential group.

Betty moved to New York City and began to regularly sing at the Apollo Theater in Harlem. In 1958, she released her first album, *Out There*. A couple of years later, the world-famous jazz trumpet player Miles Davis connected Betty with another amazing and very popular musician named Ray Charles. Betty and Ray hit it off so well that they recorded an album called *Ray Charles and Betty Carter* in 1961, which included a hit song called "Baby, It's Cold Outside." In 1963, Betty even got a chance to tour Japan with jazz great Sonny Rollins.

In addition to her singing, Betty was known to be an amazing jazz composer and arranger. She helped the careers of young jazz musicians by putting them in her band and making them work very hard. Playing with Betty was lovingly called the "Betty Carter University," as her music changed from slow to fast and from loud to soft in seconds, and her young players had to be sure to keep up.

Betty was such a great teacher that she established a summer school for young jazz musicians called the Jazz Ahead series, which was held at the John F. Kennedy Center for the Performing Arts in Washington, DC. In fact, the program still exists to this day! In 1997, a year before she died, Betty was awarded the National Medal of Arts by President Bill Clinton. What an amazing life and legacy she has left the jazz world.

Tracy Chapman

(B. MARCH 30, 1964)

FOLK

Revolutionary Singer-Songwriter

"My mother sang, my sister could sing, music was so much in the fabric of my life and upbringing."

—TRACY CHAPMAN

With her silky, low-toned voice placed over her carefully crafted guitar melodies, Tracy Chapman has become one of the most important Black women singer-songwriters of the twentieth century.

When Tracy was four years old, her mother bought her a ukulele. Tracy quickly began learning to pluck the strings. By the time she was eight, she had learned to play the guitar and was even writing her own songs. Tracy always held a torch for music while attending high school and college, but she didn't begin her impactful music career until after she graduated from school.

At twenty-three years old, Tracy signed a record deal with Elektra Records and in 1988 she released her self-titled first album. The album went on to sell millions of copies! The first single on the album was called "Fast Car," about a young woman who finds herself stuck in a small town with her struggling family, yearning to move to the city and begin a new life. Popularity came quickly to the talented folk musician after she performed at the 1988 Nelson Mandela 70th Birthday Tribute, which was aired on television all over the world that spring.

Tracy's next single, "Talkin' 'bout a Revolution," showed the world that Tracy was not just a musician but also an activist who wrote songs about serious issues like poverty and racial injustice. Her first major work as an activist started with her travels on the Amnesty International Human Rights Now! tour more than twenty years ago, and to this day Tracy continues to use her talent as a songwriter to help others and to raise awareness for equal human rights.

But Tracy also writes beautiful love songs. The third single from her first album, a romantic ballad called "Baby Can I Hold You," showed that Tracy was a well-rounded songwriter who was able to pen songs about many different emotions and subjects. This ability made her an international star who had something to say about the world around her and the contents of her heart.

Tracy's calm, mellow singing style is thoughtful and touching. She isn't the average pop star who wears shiny costumes or has a huge fleet of backup dancers and singers. Many times, Tracy plays alone onstage, leaving nothing between her and her fans but her voice and the work of her steady hands strumming and picking her guitar.

Between 1989 and 2008, Tracy released seven albums that, combined, sold more than forty million records worldwide, and which saw the success of singles like "Give Me One Reason" and "Telling Stories." In 2008, Tracy was asked to compose music for a play called *Blood Knot* by Athol Fugard.

In 2020, Tracy made her first TV appearance in more than five years on *Late Night with Seth Meyers* to sing "Talkin' 'bout a Revolution" the night before the presidential election between Joe Biden and Donald J. Trump. Tracy's songs continue to give voice to younger generations and remind the world that we don't have to be silent in times of uncertainty and unrest.

Natalie Cole

(FEBRUARY 6, 1950, TO DECEMBER 31, 2015)

R&B / JAZZ

Following in Her Father's Musical Footsteps

"I was determined to create my own identity."

—NATALIE COLE

Natalie Cole was an elegant singer who had the shimmering eyes of her father, music superstar Nat King Cole. By the time she turned eleven, she was singing and performing on her own. But it wasn't until Natalie finished college in 1972 that she began working hard on her music career and to pursue stardom.

Her first album, *Inseparable*, was released in 1975, and the world responded very well to her beautifully longing soprano voice. Two songs from this album—"This Will Be" and "Inseparable"—became hits, which helped make Natalie a rising star and won her a Grammy for Best New Artist. She recorded two more hit records shortly after: *Natalie* (1976) and *Unpredictable* (1977). Many critics thought that her second and third albums wouldn't do as well as her first, but they were proved wrong.

Although Natalie was incredibly successful—and fame came to her very quickly—she began to do drugs that made her quite sick. She worked extremely hard to recover. Natalie did get better, and in 1987, she began to release top-selling albums again. The best-selling album of her career, *Unforgettable . . . with Love*, was released in 1991. This album put her back on top, selling more than seven million copies. Natalie showed the world that sometimes you can fall and make mistakes, but if you work hard and let go of things that hurt you, you can once again attain your dreams.

In 1991, Natalie released a new arrangement of her deceased father's famous song "Unforgettable," where she and her dad, Nat King Cole, sing the song as a duet. Using new technology, producers were able to blend Natalie's and her father's voices to make it sound like they were singing together thirty years after he died. The song is a very beautiful duet and was a nice symbol of her love for her father.

Her later albums include *Ask a Woman Who Knows* (2002) and *Leavin'* (2006) and her Grammy Award–winning album *Still Unforgettable* (2008). Although Natalie didn't have an easy career or life due to drugs and illness, she *was* able to overcome her pain and lend her loving voice to her millions of admiring and adoring fans.

Elizabeth Cotten

(JANUARY 5, 1893, TO JUNE 29, 1987)

FOLK / BLUES

A True Musical Treasure

"I was just glad to get the Grammy. I didn't know what the thing was. It's the honor what I loved."

—ELIZABETH COTTEN

Elizabeth "Libba" Cotten is one of the most important folk musicians in music history. She grew up in the early 1900s and began playing her older brother's banjo at the age of seven. By the time she was nine years old, Libba was working as a servant and saved the money she earned to buy her very first guitar. She wrote her first song, the now well-known folk tune "Freight Train," in her early teen years.

Libba was a left-handed guitar player, making her stand out even more as a musical artist. Guitars are usually made for people who strum with their right hand, so Libba simply flipped the guitar upside down to pick the strings with her left hand as she played the notes on the fretboard with her right. Her style of playing, where she played the bass strings (low-sounding strings) in counterpoint to the treble strings (high-sounding strings) was eventually named the "Cotten style."

When Libba was still young, people in her church found out about her music and asked her to quit playing the guitar and writing songs because they didn't think the music she was playing was godly. Because of this, Libba actually stopped playing guitar for many years.

But then came a fateful day. While she was working in a department store in Washington, DC, Libba found a little girl who had lost her mother. Libba helped the girl eventually find her mom, who was none other than Ruth Crawford Seeger—from the famous musical Seeger family. Libba got along well with Ruth and was invited to work in the Seeger home as a maid. Libba took the job and sometimes, while working, she would quietly play the family's guitar when she didn't think anyone was listening. Ruth eventually heard Libba playing guitar, however, and told her husband, Charles, about Libba's talent. Charles was so impressed with Libba's playing that he requested to record her music.

In 1957, at sixty-two years old, Libba recorded her very first album, *Freight Train and Other North Carolina Folk Songs and Tunes*. The Seegers created opportunities for Libba to play in the homes of famous politicians, including a man who would become president: John F. Kennedy. Libba's other albums include *Shake Sugaree* (1967), *When I'm Gone* (1979), and *Elizabeth Cotten Live!* (1983), which won her a Grammy.

Elizabeth "Libba" Cotten played music until she passed away in 1987. Even though she started her musical career later in life, Libba's songwriting and guitar playing felt fresh and her songs were lovingly written. She is now an important figure in folk music history. Her style was unlike anything anyone had ever heard before and she was rewarded for being courageous enough to pursue her childhood dreams at sixty years old!

Ella Fitzgerald

(APRIL 25, 1917, TO JUNE 15, 1996)

JAZZ

The First Lady of Song / The Queen of Jazz

"The only thing better than singing is more singing."

—ELLA FITZGERALD

Jazz singer Ella Fitzgerald had a hard childhood. Her mother died when she was young, and Ella began skipping school and hanging out with the wrong crowd. But she turned her life around and grew up to become one of the most recognized and powerful jazz singers of the twentieth century.

When Ella was a teenager, she moved to Harlem to live with her aunt, and there she found her way onstage at the famous Apollo Theater. Ella sang at the theater's Amateur Night to a crowd who immediately fell in love with her stunning voice. She continued to sing as often as she could and finally won a chance to work with musician Tiny Bradshaw's band at the Harlem Opera House. Following these performances, Ella was officially discovered by bandleader and drummer Chick Webb, who hired her to sing with his band.

Once she realized that people adored her, Ella began recording songs she penned, one of which was "A-Tisket, A-Tasket," a new version of a nursery rhyme that Ella co-wrote in 1938. This song made her famous. Around the same time, Ella also became the leader of Chick Webb's band after he passed away. She renamed the band Ella Fitzgerald and Her Famous Orchestra. Ella had large ensembles of musicians playing with her while she led her band, but then a new style of jazz music emerged where a small group of musicians would improvise together, a sound called "bebop." Ella loved this exciting style of jazz! It gave her a chance to "scat," where she would sing improvised sounds to go along with the free-flowing bebop music style.

Her 1947 song "Oh, Lady Be Good!" showcased her light, breezy voice and made her even more attractive to jazz fans. In the 1950s, music began to change again, and bebop wasn't as popular as it once was. So Ella's manager, Norman Granz, had the idea that she should sing several "songbooks," which would include songs from some of the best songwriters of her time. Her first songbook, in 1956, was titled *Ella Fitzgerald Sings the Cole Porter Song Book* and it was quite successful. Following that, *Ella Fitzgerald Sings the Duke Ellington Song Book* was even more successful in 1957, as the legendary composer Ellington himself played and wrote new songs just for Ella to sing. These albums made her a very consistent artist who offered the world songs that they would remember for years to come.

Ella's stunning talent and uplifting style of singing (she could miraculously make a sad song sound happy) made her a jazz fan favorite for many decades. It has been said that Ella was actually a very shy and quiet person. She made music into the 1990s, but then became ill and could not perform for a few years before her death in 1996. Ella Fitzgerald is known as one of the best singers to have ever lived. She's *absolutely* the queen of jazz!

Roberta Flack

(B. FEBRUARY 10, 1937)

FOLK SOUL

A Master of Folk-Soul Music

*"I tell my own story in each song as honestly
as I can in the hope that each person
can hear it and feel their own story
within those feelings."*

—ROBERTA FLACK

For much of Roberta Flack's life, classical music was the way she expressed herself. Her gift for playing the piano showed promise as soon as she began to study the instrument at age nine. Growing up, Roberta gave much of her attention to music, and when she turned fifteen, she had gotten so good at playing piano that she received a full scholarship to Howard University, a historically Black college in Washington, DC. (In fact, Roberta is known to be one of the youngest people to ever enroll at the university!) She studied hard and graduated four years later. During that time, Roberta had no idea that she would eventually become an influential musician. After college, she taught music to children and gave private lessons in her home so she could afford to take care of herself.

It was her vocal teacher Frederick Wilkerson who first heard Roberta playing pop and R&B music and who encouraged her to play different kinds of music outside of the classical genre. Roberta started playing nightclubs after teaching her classes and was soon offered a job playing at a DC restaurant called Mr. Henry's. From there her name and beautiful music began to spread. Her fan base grew to include famous movie stars and filmmakers who heard about her beautiful style of R&B music.

Roberta's first recorded album, *First Take*, was released in 1969. The album didn't sell very well until movie star and film director Clint Eastwood chose one of the songs, "The First Time Ever I Saw Your Face," to be featured in his 1971 movie, *Play Misty for Me*. This lucky exposure caused the song and her first album to sell more than one million records, and it also won Roberta a Grammy for Record of the Year. The following year, she released the song she is most known for: "Killing Me Softly with His Song." This song was another huge hit and won her another Record of the Year Grammy. Roberta is the only artist to ever win Record of the Year two years in a row.

Roberta's music is simply elegant. Her soft, flowing voice coated over her minimal piano playing makes her sound very different from the pop music of the late 1960s and the disco and funk music of the 1970s. She sang about the quietness and sensitivity of love, which made her fans feel deeply connected to her music. Her music is so calming that a new kind of genre was created around her sweet and powerful musical style, called "quiet storm."

Roberta's third number-one song came in 1974 and was titled "Feel Like Makin' Love." Roberta also performed duets with singer Donny Hathaway in the 1970s and Peabo Bryson in the 1980s, and she had a big dance hit with reggae artist Maxi Priest in 1991. Her songs with other artists are just as beautiful and romantic as her solo songs, giving her ways to express her music to different listeners.

Roberta is a lifelong musician who made sweet and touching songs while the world around her was whizzing by. She is living proof that it can pay to simply be yourself while following your dream.

Aretha Franklin

(MARCH 25, 1942, TO AUGUST 16, 2018)

GOSPEL / SOUL

The Queen of Soul

*"It really is an honor if I can be inspirational to
a younger singer or person. It means I've done my job."*

—ARETHA FRANKLIN

Aretha Franklin, the incredible "Queen of Soul," is one of the most beloved singers of all time. She has sung more than one hundred hit songs, and many of those songs rose to number one in every decade since the 1960s, including "Never Gonna Break My Faith," a gospel song that was released in 2020, two years after she passed away.

Aretha was born in Memphis, Tennessee, to piano player and vocalist Barbara Siggers Franklin and a minister, C. L. Franklin, who moved her family to Detroit when Aretha was young so he could become the lead pastor of New Bethel Baptist Church.

The church is where young Aretha received much of her musical training. She sang in the church choir, and it quickly became clear to her father (her mother tragically passed away when Aretha was only nine) and the members of her church that she was a star in the making. She was encouraged to become a soloist and she learned to sing leads and stand out from the crowd.

To help after the loss of her mother, women from the church came to watch over Aretha and her siblings. One of those women was the famous gospel singer Mahalia Jackson, also known as the "Queen of Gospel." By the time Aretha was twelve, she was traveling as a singer with her father, who grew to be a famous, well-paid preacher. Aretha would spend summers with successful gospel singers like Mavis Staples's family, and she caught the attention of powerful pop musicians like Sam Cooke and Dinah Washington.

Aretha recorded albums throughout her teenage years and released her first non-gospel album, *Aretha: With the Ray Bryant Combo*, when she was only nineteen years old. In her early professional recording career, she sang in different musical styles, like jazz, blues, doo-wop, and R&B, but her sultry voice would eventually earn her the title of "Queen of Soul."

Aretha is most known for her songs "(You Make Me Feel Like) A Natural Woman," "Chain of Fools," and "I Say a Little Prayer." But her *most* famous song is one written by soul singer Otis Redding called "Respect." The way Aretha sang it from a hardworking woman's point of view made it an important song for the women's rights and civil rights movements of the 1960s. In fact, Aretha Franklin knew Dr. Martin Luther King Jr. very well because of her father, and Dr. King's influence made her a strong activist.

Aretha's music has touched generations of people and musical artists like Alicia Keys, Mariah Carey, Mary J. Blige, and Lauryn Hill. Her songs play on even today, after her death, and her beautiful spirit will shine for decades to come.

Billie Holiday

(APRIL 7, 1915, TO JULY 17, 1959)

JAZZ

The Queen of Song

"People don't understand the kind of fight it takes to record what you want to record the way you want to record it."

—BILLIE HOLIDAY

It was a long, hard road for Billie Holiday to become one of the world's most important and influential singers. Eleanora Fagan (Billie's birth name) was abused as a young person and no one truly knows who her birth father was. She moved from Baltimore to Harlem when she was a teenager. In Harlem, she began performing in nightclubs and soon received a record deal in 1935, when she was only twenty years old.

Billie's keen ability to improvise music, which meant she could sing along to music and make up her own melodies and lyrics, helped her stand out as a young vocalist. One of her earliest recordings—"What a Little Moonlight Can Do"—brought her some success, and this marked the moment when Billie was on her way to becoming the woman she was destined to be.

Billie traveled with one of the best big-band groups of the time, which was led by Count

Basie. He had a say in how the band played, making sure the music was just right for her beautiful, emotional singing. After leaving Count Basie's group because of disagreements with the band, Billie began singing with Artie Shaw's band—an all-white big band—making her the first Black woman to sing with a major all-white band.

Billie later came upon the song that would make her a legend: "Strange Fruit." The song was about the lynching of Black people, and Billie was hesitant to sing it for a long time, being afraid that people would lash out at her. But when she finally performed this transformative song, she captivated her audience, wooing them with her sad voice and the violent tone to her lyrics. The song made her a star. It did bring a lot of troubling attention due to racism, but once Billie decided to sing the song, she was determined to never let anyone keep her from performing it whenever she could.

Billie went on to have hit songs like "God Bless the Child," "Lover Man," and many others. She sold millions of records in her lifetime. But, sadly, Billie couldn't escape her complicated life. She was known to have a drug habit and eventually found herself in court, a trial she called "The United States of America versus Billie Holiday." She went to jail for drug possession but was soon released. Billie, fortunately, was able to continue her successful singing career until she passed away. Her life was cut all too short due to her inability to quit drinking and doing drugs.

Billie Holiday was a wounded soul who rose to stardom. After her death, her popularity continued to grow, and Billie's spirit lives on in the hearts and minds of the music-loving masses. She is one of the most powerful and impactful singers in all of jazz history.

Lena Horne

(JUNE 30, 1917, TO MAY 9, 2010)

JAZZ

An Icon for the Ages

"I made a promise to myself to be kinder to other people."

—LENA HORNE

For more than seventy years, Lena Horne lived her life as a singer, actress, and civil rights activist. She released more than fifty music albums, and as a movie star, she was featured in dozens of films even while segregation was still legal in the United States.

Lena was born in Brooklyn, New York. She moved around a lot as a child and was mainly raised by her grandparents because her mother was a working actress who often traveled and her father moved away when she was a little girl. When she wasn't with her grandparents, Lena split her time between her parents' houses, one in New York and the other in Pittsburgh. In Pittsburgh Lena received early training as a jazz singer by working with talented musicians like jazz pianist and composer Billy Strayhorn.

41

While in her early twenties, Lena began working as a dancer in the chorus of a very popular Black nightclub in Harlem, the Cotton Club. There she met jazz singer Adelaide Hall, who taught Lena the ins and outs of being an entertainer. Lena learned quickly and became a rising star in New York City. In 1935, she was featured in her first of many films, *Cab Calloway's Jitterbug Party*. Although things were going well for her, Lena knew there was a bigger world outside of New York, so in the 1940s she moved to Los Angeles to perform and act in movies. She is best known for singing her signature song, "Stormy Weather," in the film *Stormy Weather* in 1943.

Lena struggled in Hollywood because she was only allowed to sing in films—she couldn't have actual leading roles because she was Black. Lena was forced to sing songs that could easily be cut out of the movies she appeared in because many movie theaters in the United States refused to show movies with Black actors due to segregation and racism.

But Lena persevered and worked successfully through both World War II and the civil rights movement. During the war, she entertained the troops and would get angry because the Black soldiers had to sit in the back while she performed. Lena would walk offstage and go to the back of the room and perform as closely as she could to the Black soldiers to show them that they mattered to her. During the civil rights era, Lena spoke at the historic March on Washington in 1963 and worked with Eleanor Roosevelt to enact laws to stop Black people from being lynched.

In the 1960s and '70s, Lena appeared on many different TV shows, including *The Muppet Show* and *Sesame Street*. In the 1980s and through the '90s, she continued to act, work, and perform, even as she entered old age.

Lena Horne was known for her beauty, her grace, and her bravery as an activist who fought for equality in the face of racism and unfairness. She is an irreplaceable icon in Black music and a deeply loved figure of the twentieth century.

Janet Jackson

(B. MAY 16, 1966)

R&B / POP

The Youngest of Music's Royal Family

*"I would hope my legacy would be bringing smiles
to faces. Happiness with my music."*

—JANET JACKSON

As the youngest of ten children (including pop megastar Michael Jackson and the extraordinary R&B pop group the Jackson 5, composed of her brothers), Janet Jackson was destined to be a world-famous singer. She became that and much more, having sold more than 180 million albums across the globe as well as working as an actress throughout her long career.

Janet got her start by performing on her family's TV show, *The Jacksons*, in 1976. She would act, sing, and dance alongside her brothers and sisters who already had music careers and lots of fame. Before she signed to a record label and began releasing music at sixteen years old, Janet worked as an actor in the beloved 1970s and

'80s TV shows *Good Times*, *Diff'rent Strokes*, and *Fame*—a show that was set in a performing arts school.

It took time for Janet's music career to grow, as her first two albums, *Janet Jackson* (1982) and *Dream Street* (1984), were not as successful as her third and fourth albums, *Control* (1986) and *Janet Jackson's Rhythm Nation 1814* (1989), which sold millions of records worldwide. With *Control*, she signed on to work with producers Jimmy Jam and Terry Lewis, whose innovative music combined R&B, hip-hop, dance, and industrial (machinelike music) to create a new sound for Janet and her generation of music fans.

Control had a strong focus on girl empowerment and self-awareness with songs like "Let's Wait Awhile," "The Pleasure Principle," "Control," and "What Have You Done for Me Lately." The record sold five million copies in the United States and ten million worldwide. The music of her fourth album, *Janet Jackson's Rhythm Nation 1814*, was about speaking out for those who didn't have a voice in the world and those who suffered from poverty. Janet sang about war and gun violence and how society needs to work together to create a better world. The album was dark and serious in tone, and it showed a side of Janet Jackson that hadn't been seen before—a woman who wanted to talk about difficult topics in order to make the world a better place. This album went on to sell twelve million copies and Janet became a global superstar. Her *Rhythm Nation* tour sold out all over the world within minutes.

In 1993, Janet's acting and music careers flowed into one as she starred in the film *Poetic Justice* with rapper Tupac Shakur while releasing her fifth album, *Janet.*

In real life, Janet is known to be soft-spoken and a very private person. She is extremely smart and uses her music to inspire people to treat one another with respect. Her albums *The Velvet Rope* (1997), *All for You* (2001), *Damita Jo* (2004), *20 Y.O.* (2006), *Discipline* (2008), and *Unbreakable* (2015) all share stories of pain, hope, and healing with her fans. Janet Jackson found her voice through music so others could find their own hope and freedom.

Mahalia Jackson

(OCTOBER 26, 1911, TO JANUARY 27, 1972)

GOSPEL

The Queen of Gospel

*"When you sing gospel you have a feeling
there is a cure for what's wrong."*

—MAHALIA JACKSON

To many people around the world, there is no doubt that Mahalia Jackson is the "Queen of Gospel." She earned this title because she was close to powerful leaders of the 1960s civil rights movement and was chosen to sing at the March on Washington in 1963 to more than 200,000 people, right before Dr. Martin Luther King Jr. gave his historic "I Have a Dream" speech.

Mahalia was born in 1911 to a poor family in New Orleans. Her mother died before Mahalia was seven years old, and she had to leave school in the eighth grade to earn money for her family. She lived with her aunt Duke, who was very strict, but Aunt Duke also took her to church every Sunday, where Mahalia learned about the power of gospel music. Mahalia thought gospel

47

had a way of easing the minds and souls of others in the midst of racism and segregation. The hope and comfort she found in singing those songs followed her throughout her career.

In 1928, Mahalia moved from New Orleans to Chicago and began to sing at Greater Salem Missionary Baptist Church. Mahalia's voice was undeniably beautiful, attracting attention from Christian Black communities. In 1931, when Mahalia was twenty years old, she moved to Chicago. She quickly found a church to attend and on her first visit to Greater Salem Baptist Church she felt it in her spirit to sing "Hand Me Down My Silver Trumpet, Gabriel" in front of the entire church. After hearing this spontaneous performance, Mahalia was invited to sing with the church's choir. She toured around Chicago and nearby towns. Her voice caught the attention of gospel songwriter, composer, and "Father of Gospel Music," Thomas Dorsey, who took her under his wing. For the next five years, she traveled, singing Thomas Dorsey's songs and making a name for herself.

Along with her musical tours, she recorded nearly thirty albums over the course of her life, which allowed her music to expand beyond the poor and working-class Black communities to white Americans and gospel lovers around the globe. Her albums sold millions of copies during her lifetime. Nonetheless, because Mahalia had been poor and from the South, her heart was always connected to the struggles of the less fortunate who suffered from segregation and joblessness.

Mahalia's voice was pure and soothing. She could heal the spirits of many when she sang gospel songs and hymns like "Move On Up a Little Higher," "Go Tell It on the Mountain," "The Lord's Prayer," and "Didn't It Rain." In 1950, she gave her first performance at Carnegie Hall in New York City, a very prestigious place for singers to appear.

Even though Mahalia became a wealthy international star, she still experienced prejudice in her own life. For example, when she tried to buy a house in Chicago, white real estate agents refused to sell her one simply because she was Black. When she did settle into a house, her white neighbors shot bullets through her window! The songs she was singing about overcoming the pain of her people also guided her to have strength throughout her life.

Mahalia Jackson was a brave, compassionate, and selfless person who became one of the most powerful women in America through her music and undying service to others.

Etta James

(JANUARY 25, 1938, TO JANUARY 20, 2012)

R&B / ROCK AND ROLL

A Powerful Vocal Influencer

*"What happens is, when I perform,
I'm somewhere else. I go back in time
and get in touch with who I really am.
I forget my troubles, my worries."*

—ETTA JAMES

R&B and rock and roll singer Etta James did not have an easy childhood. A bright spot in her young life was her mother making sure Etta learned to sing at the age of five. Etta took lessons from James Earle Hines, the choirmaster at St. Paul Baptist Church in Los Angeles. James was not very nice to her, but despite that, Etta was a strong girl and developed a loud, confident singing voice.

Etta lived for a time in foster care because her mom couldn't take care of her. One of her foster mothers was also hard on Etta. She would wake up the young girl at night and make Etta sing for people during late-night parties. Throughout her life, Etta remembered the struggles of her younger years, and this often made it hard for her to perform for people on the spot.

When Etta became a teenager, her birth mom began to care for her again and moved her to San Francisco, where Etta started a girl singing group called the Creolettes in the early 1950s. When she was fourteen years old, Etta met Johnny Otis, an older musician who recognized her talent while looking for someone to sing a song called "Roll with Me, Henry," which was later renamed "The Wallflower." Johnny Otis is also the person who changed her name from Jamesetta Hawkins (the name she was born with) to Etta James.

Etta quickly rose to stardom after "The Wallflower" became an R&B hit in 1955. She toured with famous musicians of the time like Little Richard and Ike and Tina Turner. Her first major solo hit song was a romantic love song called "All I Could Do Was Cry," and in 1960 she released her first album, *At Last!*, which included another one of her popular songs, "A Sunday Kind of Love." But to this day, Etta is best known for her deeply powerful love song "At Last."

Etta made music throughout the 1960s and early 1970s, but then she stopped her growing career for about ten years because of struggles in her personal life. However, she successfully made a comeback by singing at the 1984 Summer Olympics. In the late 1980s and the 1990s, Etta returned with successful albums like *Seven Year Itch* and *Mystery Lady: Songs of Billie Holiday*.

Etta had a strong, low, bellowing voice that was sometimes gravelly and raw. Her singing style was loved by many women musicians who wanted to sing just like her. Etta James touched so many people with her voice. She will go down in history for being a vocal influence for some of the world's greatest singers today.

Chaka Khan

(B. MARCH 23, 1953)

FUNK / SOUL / JAZZ

The Queen of Funk

*"We also need to learn how to love
one another as women. How to appreciate
and respect each other."*

—CHAKA KHAN

Yvette Marie Stevens was a precocious teenager who learned about the world from her father's art community and his friends in Chicago. She had lots of freedom to go to parties and to explore the city. She learned about jazz from her grandmother, but early on Chaka found that she loved R&B music. So she started an all-girl band called the Crystallettes when she was just eleven years old!

That was only the beginning of Chaka's music career. She performed in bands around Chicago throughout her middle and high school years, but she ultimately found true fame as the seventeen-year-old lead vocalist of the mixed-race funk band Rufus. She earned a spot in the group after two members of the new band saw her cool, fun, and energetic performance while she was regularly singing with different bands around Chicago.

The group worked with the successful R&B singer-songwriter Stevie Wonder, who collaborated with them on a song he wrote for Chaka called "Tell Me Something Good." This catchy, funky song was Rufus's first major hit and it made Chaka the undoubted "Queen of Funk." The group was known for their unique and high-energy performances, led by Chaka, who became the main attraction. But not everything was so positive. There was a lot of fighting among the band, and the band was very controlling over Chaka. Eventually she signed a solo record deal and put out her first solo song, titled "I'm Every Woman." She became a top-selling artist in her own right as the popularity of her first album soared.

Chaka's voice is beautiful and electrifying, her tones high and sultry, and her smooth delivery has made her a beloved vocalist with millions of fans. She has a natural talent. Even though she never learned to read music, Chaka could sing the notes she wanted instrumentalists to play, and this shows a skill that comes from deep within her artistic, musical soul.

Since her first album, Chaka Khan has enjoyed a wonderfully successful and lengthy career. She has won many awards, toured with and recorded duets with artists like Prince and Mary J. Blige, and even been a contestant on *Dancing with the Stars*! She released her most recent album, called *Hello Happiness*, in 2019. The music on this latest album showcases her continuously positive light—a light that she has illuminated in the world for more than thirty years.

Angélique Kidjo

(B. JULY 14, 1960)

WORLD MUSIC

A Global Music Superstar

"I want to show you the links back to Africa."

—ANGÉLIQUE KIDJO

Angélique Kidjo is one of the world's biggest international music stars. She was born in Benin, a country on Africa's Atlantic coast near Nigeria, in the coastal city of Ouidah. She has eight siblings, including several brothers who played together in a band that was influenced by American soul music.

Angélique loved all kinds of music as a little girl. She enjoyed pop music from other African countries, salsa music from Cuba, and especially the traditional African music she grew up listening to with her parents.

When Angélique was six years old, she performed for the first time as part of a dance troupe. She liked being onstage so much that she started a band. Angélique was well on her way to becoming a successful musical artist, but as she got older, her country had a

57

change in political power. The leaders of Benin tried to force her to only sing political anthems for the country, but Angélique wanted to be free to live the way she pleased.

She left for Paris with hopes of becoming a lawyer, so she could help the poor people in her country find freedom, but she quickly realized music was the best way for her to touch the poor. Angélique set out on a mission to play music that would bring the world together.

She began her mission by singing and cowriting songs for several years in a French African jazz band called Pili Pili. Finally she felt ready to move on to a solo career. Her first album, *Parakou* (1990), opened doors for her to receive a major record deal, and then she released her second album, *Logozo* (1991). *Logozo* has elements of different sounds from all over the world, like Afro-funk, reggae, samba, salsa, gospel, jazz, and Congolese rumba. Her music is super unique!

Angélique continues to play music influenced by many different cultures. She's gotten so good at making diverse music that she's become one of the most powerful international music artists on the planet.

Nonetheless, Angélique hasn't forgotten about her mission to help the poor and underprivileged. She is currently the Goodwill Ambassador for the United Nations Children's Fund, an international organization that helps kids all over the world live safe and healthy lives. Angélique also started the Batonga Foundation, an important organization that ensures that girls in Africa can get an education no matter their age or class. Today Angélique continues to perform and record albums. Her prestigious music career gave her the global platform, fan base, and influence to be able to help others who were less fortunate.

Gladys Knight

(B. MAY 28, 1944)

SOUL

The Empress of Soul

"Soul is just that inner spirit. I use that inner spirit for whatever it is I do."

—GLADYS KNIGHT

Like many legendary soul singers, Gladys Knight has been singing for most of her life. In 1952, she won *The Original Amateur Hour* television show when she was just eight years old! She was already on her way to becoming a star on the day her family's record player broke at her brother's birthday party and Gladys quickly formed a group with her brother, sister, and cousins to entertain everyone at the party. The young singers were so good that Gladys's mother encouraged them to continue to sing together. That is how the incredible soul group Gladys Knight and the Pips became one of the best-known Black singing groups.

Gladys Knight and the Pips entered many talent shows around their hometown of Atlanta, Georgia, and they won every show they competed in. They even played shows as opening acts for successful older musicians like Sam Cooke and Jackie Wilson. The group scored their very first hit in 1961—a dreamy song called "Every Beat of My Heart"—and in 1967, they released one of their most influential songs, "I Heard It Through the Grapevine."

Gladys Knight and the Pips continued as a top-selling group and released their most famous song, "Midnight Train to Georgia," in 1973. They had beautiful voices that brought people together (and really cool dance steps, too). They were one of the first groups to show early hip-hop culture and dance moves, featuring them in the music video for their 1983 song "Save the Overtime (For Me)." They were unique because they were able to keep up with what was cool and to connect with young people from different generations.

After more than thirty years, some members of the Pips decided to retire, so Gladys moved on to work on her solo career. She recorded the song "Licence to Kill" for the 1989 James Bond movie of the same title. In 1991, she sang an amazing song called "Superwoman"—and who better to sing such a song than a superwoman herself!

Now in her late seventies, Gladys Knight has been performing and recording music for more than sixty years. People love her bubbly personality and her big, soulful voice. It takes a very special woman to make music for so many years. Gladys is certainly a special woman and an incredible artist.

Patti LaBelle

(B. MAY 24, 1944)

R&B / SOUL

The Godmother of Soul

"So if diva means giving your best, then yes, I guess I am a diva."

—**PATTI LABELLE**

P atti LaBelle has a glistening high soprano voice that rises and falls like the wings of an eagle. She is known for her heartfelt expression in the song "Wind Beneath My Wings" and her transcendent version of Judy Garland's "Over the Rainbow."

Patti grew up in a family where her parents didn't get along. It was very hard on her brothers and sisters, but twelve-year-old Patti found an outlet for her sorrow by singing in church. At age sixteen, she entered a talent show and won, which opened doors for her to sing in a group called the Ordettes. The group showed that they were good enough to record albums, with Patti as their lead singer.

Patti, however, wasn't treated very well because her skin was dark and she wasn't considered to be as beautiful as most singers (which is not the truth!). But she rose above the harshness of the music industry and proved to the world that she was beautiful and loved even if a few powerful people didn't think so.

The Ordettes' name was eventually changed to Patti LaBelle and the Blue Belles, and in 1963 the group released their first hit song, "Down the Aisle," followed by another hit in 1964 called "You'll Never Walk Alone." As 1970 approached, the group was asked to change their look and sound to mirror the new music craze—disco. Patti's group started to wear shiny makeup and glamorous silver costumes similar to those worn by rock stars David Bowie and Elton John. They also shortened the name of their group to Labelle. Their first albums *Labelle* and *Moon Shadow* were released in 1971 and 1972, but it was their third album, 1974's *Nightbirds*, that would become their most successful. On the album was the song they are best known for, "Lady Marmalade." The song sold more than one million copies and launched Patti to a new level of success.

Labelle released two more albums, called *Phoenix* and *Chameleon*, but the group began to fight, and because of this, Patti felt like it was time to start a solo career.

Patti is a dynamic and exciting entertainer. The world quickly took to her solo music and loved how she waved her arms and swayed while singing passionately. Patti picks up her microphone stand and swings it over her shoulders, smiling and singing to her audiences and telling them stories about her family and the happy and sad times in her life. The song "You Are My Friend" has become her signature recording.

Patti has recorded several great albums and has also showcased her ability as an actress by performing in the Broadway musical *Your Arms Too Short to Box with God*. In 1986, her album *Winner in You* was number one in America and sold millions of copies. Throughout the 1990s and 2000s, Patti continued to record albums and wow fans with her stage presence. Recently, she has also starred in popular shows like *Dancing with the Stars* and *The Masked Singer*.

In recent years, Patti has enjoyed running a successful business selling her delicious sweet potato pies, which fly off the shelves! She's not only a music icon and superstar, but she's actually feeding her fans as well.

Abbey Lincoln

(AUGUST 6, 1930, TO AUGUST 14, 2010)

JAZZ

An Iconic Songwriter and Actress

*"When everything is finished in a world,
the people go to look for what the artists leave.
It's the only thing that we have really in
this world—is an ability to express ourselves
and say, 'I was here.'"*

—ABBEY LINCOLN

Jazz singer and songwriter Abbey Lincoln—whose birth name was Anna Marie Wooldridge—grew up on a farm in rural Michigan with a very big family. She had eleven brothers and sisters! Her parents owned a piano and she learned to play as a little girl. Abbey liked music so much that she began to perform at both school and church.

Little did she or anyone know that she would grow up to become a legend in the world of jazz!

As she grew older, Abbey's favorite singers—Billie Holiday, Sarah Vaughan, and Dinah Washington—influenced how she sang, but she naturally became an expressive, talented singer in her own right. When she was in her twenties, she began to travel to places like California, Chicago, and even Hawaii to sing in nightclubs and to perfect her art.

In 1956 Abbey was offered an acting role to play a singer in the film *The Girl Can't Help It*, and she also released her very first album, *Abbey Lincoln's Affair . . . A Story of a Girl in Love* in 1957. She was well on her way to success and stardom, but she really began making a name for herself when, the same year, she moved to New York City and met her husband, a jazz drummer named Max Roach.

Not only did Abbey and Max love each other, but they also played music together throughout the late 1950s and during the civil rights movement of the 1960s. As a response to the unfairness of racism at this time in history, Abbey sang on Max's album *We Insist! Max Roach's Freedom Now Suite*, which has become a very famous piece of music. Abbey released nearly thirty albums as the leader of her own band as well, and she recorded two albums of the music of Billie Holiday called *Abbey Sings Billie*. Her albums *Abbey Is Blue* (1959), *Golden Lady* (1981), and *Abbey Sings Abbey* (2007) helped establish her as a true jazz master and songwriter. Her music is deep and emotional and the many albums she was able to record throughout her life leave a legacy that the world can look at to help remember her strength and talent.

Abbey Lincoln changed the jazz genre by being an honest and powerful songwriter who didn't give in to the pressure of singing sad songs about love. She wrote happy songs as well as liberating pieces of music about her culture and the world around her.

Darlene Love

(B. JULY 26, 1941)

R&B / POP

The Reemerging Star

*"I'm always happy to be a part of history.
When you're a part of history,
you live forever."*

—DARLENE LOVE

Pop singer Darlene Wright has one of the greatest comebacks in music history. Darlene's story begins in Los Angeles, where she grew up. Like many successful singers, she got her early training in a church choir.

Darlene loved music so much that by the time she was in high school, she joined a band called the Echoes, which later provided her the chance to sing with a 1960s girl group called the Blossoms. Darlene jumped at the opportunity to work with one of the world's most famous music producers, Phil Spector, with the Blossoms. She had such a beautiful voice that many famous musicians wanted her to sing on their albums—from Elvis Presley to the Beach Boys and Sonny and Cher! She also recorded her most memorable song, "Christmas (Baby Please Come Home)" while working with Spector.

Her singing career soared in the 1960s, but things began to slow down as the years marched on. When Darlene sang the lead for a hit song, "He's a Rebel" in 1962, her producer decided to tell the world that the song was performed by another group, causing her to lose a big opportunity and money as the singer of such a popular song.

As her singing gigs began to dry up, Darlene found herself working odd jobs like cleaning houses just to make ends meet. But through it all, she kept singing whenever she could. It would be more than ten years before Darlene was rediscovered by guitar player Steven Van Zandt of Bruce Springsteen's E Street Band. She was playing a show in a club in Los Angeles where Steven was in the audience. He liked her performance so much that he asked her to move to New York City to begin working regularly as a singer and actor.

Darlene decided to give New York a chance and soon landed a job singing in the musical *Leader of the Pack* in the 1980s. Her biggest job, though, was her performance of her twenty-year-old hit song "Christmas (Baby Please Come Home)" on the popular show *Late Night with David Letterman*. She would go on to sing this song on the show every year for nearly twenty years! In 2015 she even recorded a new album—*Introducing Darlene Love*—and she continues to sing and perform to this day.

Barbara Lynn

(B. JANUARY 16, 1942)

BLUES

A Soulful Electric Guitarist

*"I decided that playing piano was a little bit too common,
you know what I mean?"*

—BARBARA LYNN

Blues musician Barbara Lynn was interested in music from the time she was a little girl. Her parents played blues songs and danced around the house together, giving Barbara a peek into how much soul and rock and roll music could bring joy to anyone who listened.

When she was very young, Barbara Lynn Ozen would use her windowsill as a keyboard while she pretended to play an imaginary piano. She soon started real piano lessons and began writing poems, setting them to music. But when she turned twelve, she saw blues and pop stars like B.B. King and Elvis Presley performing on TV, and she became fascinated with the guitar. She also had it in her mind that she wanted to play something unusual. She admired Black women singers like Etta James and Ruth Brown and had seen women playing piano and singing on TV, but she hadn't seen a Black woman playing guitar.

So, Barbara began her guitar journey by playing a ukulele, and once she got good at that, her mother bought her a guitar.

While still in grade school, Barbara learned to play her electric guitar and started a band called Bobbi Lynn and Her Idols. Her band won talent shows and impressed crowds. People were excited to see a Black girl electric guitarist leading her own band. In high school, she played in an all-girl group but soon realized the other girls in the band didn't want to grow up to be music stars like she did. That made Barbara decide to make music on her own, and by the time she was twenty years old, in 1962, she had a hit song on the radio called "You'll Lose a Good Thing." The song's success made Barbara Lynn a famous musician and gave her the opportunity to tour with big stars of the time like Ike and Tina Turner, Marvin Gaye, and James Brown. She released myriad albums like *Sister of Soul* in 1964, *Here Is Barbara Lynn* in 1968, and five more between the 1980s and 2000s.

Barbara set her mind to becoming a successful musician from an early age, and she did just that. She has continued to play music well into her seventies and still inspires Black women guitarists to follow their dreams and to be themselves!

Rita Marley

(B. JULY 25, 1946)

REGGAE

The Queen of Reggae

*"It doesn't matter what color or who you are,
just know that you are a shining star, and you can
do or be anything you want to be!"*

—RITA MARLEY

Alfarita Constania Anderson (Rita Marley) met her future husband, Bob, during her budding music career in the mid-1960s. As a teenager, Rita formed a musical group called the Soulettes and quickly after, the popular reggae singer and member of the Wailers, Bob Marley, caught wind of her music and became the group's manager. As Rita and Bob worked together, they realized that they were in love. This not only heightened Rita's life as a singer, but it also sparked the journey of a reggae royal family and gave her the chance to serve her community and the world throughout her life.

At the time they met, Bob was in a successful reggae group called the Wailers, who worked on songs with the Soulettes. Both groups are featured on the song "That Ain't Right," and the Soulettes recorded several amazing songs on their own, like "Time for Everything" and "One More Chance."

Rita's music career was running smoothly, but there was a time when she had to step in and become a member of the Wailers after one of the original members, Bunny, was sent to jail. Rita fit right in, however. Her voice was sweet and supple. She was very good at singing with other people, knowing how to blend her vocals while still standing out with her unique voice.

When Rita was young, she didn't know she was going to be a reggae star. She loved to sing for her father and won a vocal music competition called Lanamans Children's Hour when she was a little girl, but Rita had planned on becoming a nurse. However, life had bigger plans for her, as her husband became an international star, bringing her onstage in front of thousands of people. Bob and Rita later formed a group together called the I-Threes, and they both went on to have successful solo music careers, sharing their lives as husband and wife and the parents of six children.

Rita and Bob had rocky points in their marriage, but Rita remained graceful and didn't let the world know that this made her sad. One of the hardest parts of her life was when Bob died of cancer in 1981. While the world grieved, Rita turned their home into a museum to honor her late husband, so that people all over the planet could always remember Bob's huge influence on music and reggae.

Rita Marley has so much love in her heart that she's also adopted thirty-five children in Ethiopia and has helped hundreds of children get a proper music education. She has won many awards for the good things she's done for children and elderly people in Jamaica, Ghana, and Ethiopia.

While spreading her generosity to others, Rita continued to make music through the 1990s and 2000s. She still travels all over the world performing and sharing her beautiful life with her adoring fans. Rita is a philanthropist and friend to many. She is a great mother and rightfully holds the crown as "Queen of Reggae."

MC Lyte

(B. OCTOBER 11, 1970)

HIP-HOP

A Pioneer Woman in Hip-Hop

*"When I get involved, I give it my heart. I mean my mind,
my soul, my body: I mean every part."*

—MC LYTE

In 1988, MC Lyte became the first woman in music history to release a full-length hip-hop album, titled *Lyte as a Rock*. Lana Michele Moorer started rapping at twelve years old, learning the ropes of the hip-hop world from her brothers, who had formed the rap group Audio Two (they eventually rapped on their sister's first three albums). Before she was a teenager, MC Lyte wrote "I Cram to Understand U (Sam)," which was about a woman who was in a relationship with someone addicted to drugs. It is known to be the first song to talk about the painful presence of a powerful drug called crack that was hurting Black communities all over America.

MC Lyte continued to be a powerful voice for her community. She was a trusted spokesperson for the Stop the Violence campaign, which promoted antiviolence to young people. She also showed her support for the Rock the Vote campaign and was the very first rapper to play New York City's famous Carnegie Hall, which came about through her activism in support of those who were suffering from AIDS, a disease that was spreading quickly and widely in the United States in the 1980s. In 1989, at nineteen years old, MC Lyte released her second album, *Eyes on This*, which featured the song "Cappuccino"—the lyrics of which stood up against violence. MC Lyte did her best to keep from cursing in her music because she knew that young people were listening. She wanted to be a role model whom kids could really listen to.

Her 1991 album, *Act Like You Know*, had a more R&B sound, adding a melodic style to her music, but in 1993, her next album, *Ain't No Other*, had a tougher hip-hop sound. The album opened with words from the iconic rapper KRS-One. A year later, MC Lyte toured with Janet Jackson and performed sold-out shows to many enthusiastic crowds.

In the late 1990s MC Lyte began to expand her career beyond the music stage, acting in TV shows like *New York Undercover* and *Moesha*. In 2000, she even became the voice of a talking doll named Tia!

MC Lyte opened doors for young girls and women to take their rightful place in the very male-dominated hip-hop music world. Even though she is a strong and commanding voice in her music, MC Lyte is also known to be very quiet and kind when offstage. She does her very best to think of the new generation of kids and loves to help any positive cause she can to make the world safer and the future brighter. In 2020, she acted in the film *Sylvie's Love*, which is a beautiful story about a woman who falls in love with a jazz musician. MC Lyte continues to share her talents by merging her music, acting, and entrepreneurial efforts to foster a diverse and successful career that will move forward well into the future!

Memphis Minnie

(JUNE 3, 1897, TO AUGUST 6, 1973)

BLUES

The Queen of Country Blues

*"I have sat and watched [the] evening sun go down.
People saying it's sad, not even a friend around."*

—MEMPHIS MINNIE

Memphis Minnie—whose given name was Lizzie Douglas—was nicknamed "kid" by her large family (her mom, dad, and twelve siblings). She learned to play the banjo when she was ten and the guitar when she was eleven. She ran away from home at the age of thirteen to play in the famous music and cultural scene of Beale Street in Memphis, Tennessee, where she performed under the name Kid Douglas.

Her musical talent shone and her sidewalk gigs earned her a job traveling with the Ringling Bros. Circus. Memphis Minnie essentially grew up in the circus, and when she was an adult, she married a few times. Her second husband, Joe McCoy, was a musician as well, and they seemed to be a musical match made in heaven as they played together and eventually received a record deal. Their record label, Columbia, decided it would be good to name them Kansas Joe and Memphis Minnie, and that's how the duo played for many years. One of their earlier recordings was of Minnie's popular song "Bumble Bee." By 1935, when Minnie was nearly thirty-eight, she had become a successful musician in Chicago and got a lot of work playing shows and making records.

Memphis Minnie had a deep and bellowing voice laid over her fingerpicking folk- and country-style guitar playing. She is regarded as the "Queen of Country Blues," due mostly to her most popular song, "Me and My Chauffeur Blues." Her guitar playing sounds happy and lighthearted, but Minnie's voice is powerful, and her lyrics are sometimes based on misfortune, loss, and sadness (as many blues songs are). The poet Langston Hughes once saw Memphis Minnie play and expressed that she had a "hard and strong voice." It was a voice that allowed her to attract fans who wanted to hear a confident woman sing her own songs.

During the 1940s Minnie began to play the electric guitar, which made her stand out from the growing crowd of Black women singer-songwriters. She opened the doors for electric guitar players like Barbara Lynn to become successful in their music careers. Memphis Minnie is an icon who made unique music. She mixed country, folk, and blues to create her songs. She played music until she grew old and was physically unable to pick up the guitar. Memphis Minnie died in 1973 and since then, country and blues lovers have never forgotten the mark she has made on music history.

Odetta

(DECEMBER 31, 1930, TO DECEMBER 2, 2008)

FOLK-SOUL

The Queen of American Folk

*"The blues is a celebration because when you take sorrow
and turn it into music, you transform it."*

—ODETTA

American folk singer Odetta was admired by many musicians throughout her career. Her music absolutely changed people's lives and opened the doors for many younger musicians to learn how to play folk. Whether it was a young Janis Joplin learning to sing like Odetta or Dr. Martin Luther King Jr. calling her the "queen of American folk music," Odetta shined a light everywhere she went, leaving an impact on people all over the world. Folk singer Bob Dylan traded in his electric guitar for an acoustic one after hearing her 1957 debut album, *Odetta Sings Ballads and Blues*. He studied her music and learned every song on the album.

Odetta Holmes took voice lessons and learned how to sing opera when she was thirteen years old. She also studied music in college in Los Angeles and landed a job in musical theater at Turnabout Theatre in 1944. She then performed in a touring production of the musical *Finian's Rainbow* in 1949 when she was nineteen years old.

Odetta didn't fall in love with folk music until she found herself feeling right at home in the coffee shops of San Francisco, where artists and musicians gathered to play guitar, read poetry, and make art. She was so inspired by this artistic scene that she decided to record her own music and released *Odetta Sings Ballads and Blues* and another album called *At the Gate of Horn* in 1957. Her 1963 record *Odetta Sings Folk Songs* became the bestselling folk album of the year, launching Odetta into a world of fame and opportunity. But her work and music went much deeper than simply attracting adoring fans.

Odetta often sang spirituals and "work songs" that enslaved and imprisoned Black people sang while they were laboring and dreaming of freedom. She was referred to as "the voice of the civil rights movement" because of her dedication to singing songs of love and liberation for her community. Civil rights leader Rosa Parks was said to be one of her biggest fans.

Odetta's voice sounded like deep cries of joy and sorrow, and she touched people's hearts and souls. Along with recording and performing music live, Odetta was also able to touch people by playing songs on TV. Her most notable appearance came in 1963 on *Tonight with Belafonte*. Harry Belafonte was a handsome and very popular Black actor and singer who gave Odetta a big opportunity by putting her on his show. She performed a song by herself and then one with Harry. Their duet was called "There's a Hole in My Bucket," and the recording sold more copies in the United Kingdom than in the United States. Odetta's music was beginning to travel around the globe.

Not only was Odetta loved by many musicians, but she also often dedicated her music to musicians she loved as well. She recorded songs by Bob Dylan for her album *Odetta Sings Dylan* in 1965, and in 1998 she released *To Ella*, an album named in memory of her friend Ella Fitzgerald, who had died two years earlier. Her album *Blues Everywhere I Go* featured songs she loved from Black women blues musicians of the 1920s and '30s.

Odetta was a tall, stately, and kind woman. She didn't wear makeup or put chemicals in her hair. She knew she was naturally beautiful. She is known to be one of the most important folk musicians of all time. Music wouldn't be the same without the gifts Odetta shared and the love she offered to the Black community.

The Pointer Sisters

(GROUP ACTIVE 1970 TO PRESENT)

R&B / POP

Trailblazers in Country Music

"We just shook everything we could shake."

—RUTH POINTER

As daughters of a preacher, Bonnie, June, Anita, and Ruth Pointer spent their early days singing gospel music. Their parents were very strict about the music the girls listened to, banning them from bringing non-Christian music into their family's home. But when their parents weren't around, the sisters enjoyed listening to R&B and rock and roll. The girls' mother allowed them to bring Elvis Presley's music into the house despite strict rules against popular music because even their mother enjoyed Presley's romantic gospel-like song "Crying in the Chapel." (Fun fact: nearly twenty years later, Elvis Presley would become a fan of the Pointer Sisters and would record a version of their 1974 hit country song "Fairytale.")

The Pointer Sisters started out as a duo with Bonnie and June. In 1969 the two performed in nightclubs under the name Pointers, a Pair, but they soon after grew into a trio when their sister Anita joined. The trio was talented enough to sign a record deal with Atlantic Records, but they were unsuccessful in producing a hit song on their own. Instead, the three sisters became successful performing as backup singers for famous artists like Elvin Bishop and Grace Slick. More opportunities arose, however, when they signed a new record deal with Blue Thumb Records and added their other sister, Ruth, to the group in 1972.

Their first album—called *The Pointer Sisters*—was released in 1973 and scored a hit song with their single "Yes We Can Can." Their fans loved them because they not only were great singers who could perform many different types of music, like country, dance, jazz, and R&B, but they also had an incredible fashion sense. June, Bonnie, Anita, and Ruth wore vintage clothes from the 1940s, which gave them a very different look from other artists in the 1970s and '80s.

Their 1974 album *That's a Plenty* had a jazz sound, but there was one song that really stood out: it was a country love song they recorded in Nashville called "Fairytale." Anita had fallen in love with a radio DJ who couldn't love her back the way she dreamed he would. So, Anita wrote the song with Bonnie and to their surprise, it became a hit! The song was so good, in fact, that they won a Grammy for Best Country Vocal Performance by a Duo or Group for it and were the very first Black women to sing at the famous country music venue Grand Ole Opry.

The Pointer Sisters recorded *Live at the Opera House* in 1974 and *Steppin'* in 1975. Bonnie decided to leave the group shortly after to pursue a solo career, but Anita, June, and Ruth went on to have a very successful career throughout the 1980s. Their songs "He's So Shy," "I'm So Excited," and "Automatic" are some of their best-known hits.

Sadly, Bonnie and June Pointer have passed away. Today, Ruth's daughter, Issa, and granddaughter, Sadako, travel with Ruth as the new Pointer Sisters, sharing the original sisters' love and legacy with their many adoring fans.

Leontyne Price

(B. FEBRUARY 10, 1927)

CLASSICAL

Prima Donna of the Century

"The ultimate of being successful is the luxury of giving yourself the time to do what you want to do."

—LEONTYNE PRICE

Leontyne Price began playing piano at the age of five in her hometown of Laurel, Mississippi. It wasn't until she was fourteen years old, however, that she discovered the majestic world of the opera. She was taken to see famed African American opera vocalist Marian Anderson sing on a school trip, and her life was never the same. After seeing Marian's performance, Leontyne knew it was her path in life to sing classical and contemporary operas.

Leontyne did well in college and with financial help from a white family whom her aunt worked for, the Chisholms, she was able to afford to go to the renowned Juilliard School, where she studied the finer points of opera singing.

It soon became clear to others that Leontyne had an incredible talent, particularly when she sang the part of Mistress Ford in Verdi's *Falstaff* while at Juilliard. Soon after, she found herself singing on Broadway as Bess in George Gershwin's *Porgy and Bess*. She toured America and Europe with the show, launching her career as an international singer.

Leontyne continued to reach large audiences, becoming the first Black person to sing a lead role on TV on NBC's *Opera Theatre*. She sang in Puccini's *Tosca*, as Pamina in *The Magic Flute* in 1956, as Madame Lidoine in *Dialogues of the Carmelites* in 1957, and as Donna Anna in *Don Giovanni* in 1960. In 1957, she sang Antonio Ghislanzoni and Giuseppe Verdi's opera *Aida* for the first time at the May Festival in Ann Arbor, Michigan. Her role in *Aida* is Leontyne's best known.

Leontyne was regarded as a very successful Black woman in the mostly white world of opera. This doesn't mean she didn't experience troubles from the racism of segregation and the boycotting of her performances while she toured the American South. But Leontyne had an outlet in traveling the globe, sharing her beautiful voice with her fans in Europe, Australia, and India.

Leontyne's greatest accomplishment came when she was asked to perform the leading role in American composer Samuel Barber's new opera *Antony and Cleopatra*, which was written for the 1966 grand opening of the Metropolitan Opera House at Lincoln Center in New York City. Barber wrote the part of Cleopatra just for Leontyne's stunning voice. She went on to continue performing in operas until the mid-1980s.

In 1997, Leontyne wrote a children's book called *Aida*. And in 2001, at seventy-four years old, she sang a concert to mourn the loss of the victims of the September 11 attacks. Her forty-plus-year career was grounded in her earthy presence, strong work ethic, and in her never doubting that her place in the opera world was truly needed and wonderfully profound. Leontyne Price's talent was undeniable and broke ground for Black women in opera and classical music.

Queen Latifah

(B. MARCH 18, 1970)

HIP-HOP / JAZZ

The Hip-Hop Queen of Queens

*"Every woman is a queen,
and we all have different things to offer."*

—QUEEN LATIFAH

Queen Latifah is an influential Black woman who has many talents. She is best known for being a female rapper who was a role model for Black girls who wanted to be seen as individuals and recognized for their intelligence.

Born Dana Owens, the young girl knew by age eight that she was meant to have a name that represented who she was inside. Dana searched through a book of Arabic names and landed on Latifah, which means "very kind." Years later her chosen name would go down in history, highlighting her hard work as a rapper, singer, and actress who gave women a voice in hip-hop culture.

In 1988, Queen Latifah became a beatboxer (someone who makes hip-hop beats with their mouth) for a group called Ladies Fresh in New York City, and she recorded her first song, "Princess of the Posse," to highlight her rap skills. People connected with her early music and in 1989, Queen Latifah signed a record deal and released her first album, *All Hail the Queen*. From that album came the song "Ladies First," which featured another woman rapper, Monie Love. The song celebrated the history and power of Black women and became a hit. Queen Latifah had strength and confidence as a rapper and challenged people to do the right thing when faced with struggle and pain.

Her 1993 album, *Black Reign*, offered the rap world a message that Black women deserve respect, speaking directly to men who called women names, physically hurt them, or treated them as if they were not equals. She released a song called "Just Another Day" that featured her silky singing voice. Queen Latifah loved singing and surprised her fans with the release of a jazz album called *The Dana Owens Album* in 2004.

Queen Latifah is a multitalented, self-aware woman who balanced an acting career alongside her musical projects. She has given homage to Black women in music who came before her by playing Bessie Smith (in the film *Bessie*) and Hattie McDaniel (in the TV miniseries *Hollywood*). She is well-known for her starring role in the 1990s comedy TV show *Living Single*. In 2007, she released the album *Trav'lin' Light*.

With all her awards, successful albums, films, and TV shows, Queen Latifah always finds a way to raise the voice and presence of Black women. She is humble and full of deep understanding of the importance of her portrayals of strong Black women to making the world a better place for future generations of Black girls. Her life truly shows that it's okay to be tough and kind at the same time.

Ma Rainey

(APRIL 26, 1886, TO DECEMBER 22, 1939)

SOUL

Mother of the Blues

"This be an empty world without the blues."

—MA RAINEY

Unlike many women singers who chose their stage names at the beginning of their careers, Gertrude Pridgett didn't officially *become* Ma Rainey until she married her husband, Will Rainey, in 1904. The couple traveled and performed as Ma and Pa Rainey after Ma had already had some success as a performer.

Ma Rainey's birthplace and childhood are a bit of a mystery, but what is known is that she started her professional career in 1900, performing at the Springer Opera House in Columbus, Georgia. Her performance was with a stage show called *The Bunch of Blackberries*. This led Ma to travel and sing with vaudeville troupes, which she did through much of her career. (Vaudeville was a type of variety show that had many different performers who played songs, danced, and did comedy routines.)

The first time Ma heard country-blues music was while she was traveling with a troupe in 1902. A woman appeared onstage with a guitar and played a deep, bluesy song that was completely different from the upbeat, jolly music heard in most vaudeville performances. Ma heard more of this soulful, country-style folk music as she toured the South. This inspired her to mix vaudeville-style music with country blues, effectively creating the style of blues music we hear to this day.

After her time performing with her husband in Tolliver's Circus and Musical Extravaganza and as Rainey and Rainey, Assassinators of the Blues, Ma Rainey set out to create her own traveling show called Madam Gertrude Ma Rainey and Her Georgia Smart Set. She then moved to Chicago to record her own collection of blues songs. She worked extremely hard and recorded at least ninety-two songs between 1923 and 1928!

Ma Rainey was an exhilarating woman who had a mouth full of gold teeth and wore fancy jewelry around her neck when she performed. She didn't care what anyone thought of her and she also became an early icon in the LGBTQ community. She is known to have discovered Bessie Smith, who earned the title of "Empress of Blues."

In the early 1930s, Ma Rainey performed small concerts and intimate shows, but she retired in 1935. She passed away in 1939. She will now and forever be considered the true "Mother of the Blues."

Minnie Riperton

(NOVEMBER 8, 1947, TO JULY 12, 1979)

R&B / POP

A Shining Star Gone Too Soon

*"Your wealth can be stolen,
but the precious riches buried deep in
your soul cannot."*

—MINNIE RIPERTON

Minnie Riperton's beautiful music took the world by storm with her signature love song, "Lovin' You." As a child living in Chicago, Minnie studied dance, but her parents recognized that she had a lovely singing voice. They wanted to nurture her singing, so they sent her to study at the prestigious Lincoln Center in Chicago. There, she focused on classical music and did very well. Her teacher wanted Minnie to become an opera singer, but the young girl fell in love with soul, R&B, and pop music, and subsequently decided to join an all-girl group called the Gems when she was fifteen years old. Singing with the Gems afforded Minnie many opportunities. She sang in other groups, too, such as the

Girls Three and the Starlets, and she also became a backup singer on the hit Fontella Bass song "Rescue Me."

While working as a receptionist at Chess Records, Minnie was asked to be in a new group called Rotary Connection. She agreed, recording and performing with the band from 1967 to 1971. This group released beautiful psychedelic soul music. Working very diligently in many groups finally paid off when Minnie was able to record her first solo album, called *Come to My Garden*, in 1970. The album had some success but not as much as she would have liked. Minnie then decided to focus on having a family (fun fact: she is the mother of comedian Maya Rudolph), but was convinced some years later to return to her music career. She couldn't refuse, and recorded her most successful album, *Perfect Angel*, in 1974, with the guidance and production expertise of iconic musician Stevie Wonder.

The album included her hit song "Lovin' You." The world responded lovingly, and the song sold more than one million copies! Her next album, 1975's *Adventures in Paradise*, also did very well, and Minnie followed that album with *Stay in Love* in 1977.

A few years later, Minnie got the news that she had cancer, but this didn't slow her down. She released her final album, *Minnie*, in 1979, the same year she died. And instead of hiding her illness, Minnie became a public spokesperson for the American Cancer Society, leading her to be honored with a Courage Award by President Jimmy Carter. Minnie *did* indeed have courage and strength, and she continued to play music until she passed away at the young age of thirty-one.

Minnie's voice was like no other. In classical music, her vocal range was coloratura soprano. She could sing very high, to the point where her voice sounded like a high-pitched whistle. Her "whistle register" made her unique. It sounded like she had a vocal superpower!

Minnie's songs were deeply romantic and dreamy and her contribution to music history will never be forgotten. Although she didn't release as many albums as other Black women singers, her legacy lives on as she lived her life courageously and with loving humility.

Diana Ross

(B. MARCH 26, 1944)

POP / SOUL

A Motown Legend

*"You can't just sit there and wait
for people to give you that golden dream.
You've got to get out there
and make it happen for yourself."*

—DIANA ROSS

Born in Detroit, Michigan, Diana Ross (whose given name was Diane) is best known as the lead singer of the 1960s pop-soul group the Supremes, who are to this day the most successful girl group of all time. The Supremes sold millions of records with hits like "Stop! In the Name of Love," "Come See About Me," "Baby Love," and "Where Did Our Love Go." They were also the top-selling musical act at the powerful Motown record label, a label known for releasing some of the most successful Black pop, R&B, and soul groups in history. With the help of Motown's owner, Berry Gordy Jr., the Supremes took the world by storm. They were just as popular as the Beatles!

Even though Diana led a successful group, she was destined for the spotlight as a solo artist. She left the Supremes in 1970 and ventured into the world as an individual woman. That year she released her first solo album, *Diana Ross*, and scored a hit song, "Ain't No Mountain High Enough."

Diana's voice sounds like a feeling of floating on a bed of clouds. She sings with a soft soprano voice that rings like a well-crafted copper bell, making it hard to deny the beauty she brings to each song she sings.

This songbird was also an actress. In 1972, Diana played the legendary jazz singer Billie Holiday in *Lady Sings the Blues*, and then she starred in a romantic movie called *Mahogany* in 1975. She sang that movie's theme song, "Theme from Mahogany (Do You Know Where You're Going To)," which became another of her hits. Diana also played Dorothy alongside a young Michael Jackson in the movie version of *The Wiz* in 1978. Because of her magnificent success in the 1960s and '70s, she was named Female Entertainer of the Century by *Billboard* magazine.

Diana continues to have a great career by recording music, acting, and performing for huge crowds. At the age of seventy-six, she received even more recognition and success when, in 2020, producer Eric Kupper remixed "Ain't No Mountain High Enough" and "I'm Coming Out / Upside Down." With more than forty years of experience, Diana Ross has built a legacy of strength, divahood, and superstar power. She paved the way for many Black women musicians who love glamour and decadence.

Jill Scott

(B. APRIL 4, 1972)

R&B / NEO-SOUL

A Sultry Star of Soul

"You owe it to yourself to live beautifully. And I am."

—JILL SCOTT

Jill Scott has a soothing and mesmerizing voice that brought an earthy sound to the R&B and hip-hop worlds. After deciding that teaching high school English was not the perfect path for her, Jill began to perform at open mics (these are events where anyone can go up onstage and perform) to share her voice, poetry, and songwriting with audiences in Philadelphia. Through performing, Jill earned the admiration of hip-hop drummer Ahmir "Questlove" Thompson of the hip-hop group the Roots.

Jill was invited to a recording studio to write songs with Questlove, and they came up with a hip-hop love song called "You Got Me." Fellow soul singer Erykah Badu sang Jill's lyrics on "You Got Me" and the song gained popularity with fans. Even though Jill wasn't on the recording, she did sing the song with the Roots in a live performance—and her career took off from there.

Jill's first album, *Who Is Jill Scott? Words and Sounds Vol. 1*, was released in 2000. It featured a rootsy and soulful song called "A Long Walk," which brought Jill great success. Her career grew with her second album, *Beautifully Human: Words and Sounds Vol. 2*, and while she loved to sing and write songs, she always kept poetry at the center of her heart. In 2005, she released a book of poetry called *The Moments, the Minutes, the Hours*.

Jill has a particularly unique way of making her words flow like a peaceful river. Although she is a talented writer, she also loves to sing songs written by other talented women. In 2007, she sang a Grammy-winning version of "God Bless the Child," which was written by Billie Holiday, alongside musicians George Benson and Al Jarreau.

She recorded additional albums over the years—*The Real Thing: Words and Sounds Vol. 3* (2007), *The Light of the Sun* (2011), and *Woman* (2015). *Woman* became a number one hit record, touching the world with its empowering and sensuous neo-soul songs. Jill Scott comes from the lineage of amazing Black women singers whose voice stood out from the crowd, staying deeply entrenched in her beautiful expressions of love, heartache, and the experience of being a Black woman.

Nina Simone

(FEBRUARY 21, 1933, TO APRIL 21, 2003)

SOUL / JAZZ

The High Priestess of Soul

"I feel what they feel. And people who listen to me know that, and it makes them feel like they're not alone."

—NINA SIMONE

The larger-than-life, deep, husky, powerful voice of Nina Simone continues to be an inspiration to young people and the world's best musicians to this day. Nina was different. Very different. She was a classically trained piano player who wouldn't stand for the injustice of racism throughout her entire life. She became an outspoken civil rights activist who sang songs that railed against the mistreatment of American Black communities.

When Nina was eleven, she played her first recital at the Tryon Library in Tryon, North Carolina. While in attendance, her parents were asked to sit in the back of the room because Black people weren't allowed to sit in the front of any public places or on buses (as well as being forced to use separate bathrooms from white patrons). This was the law in America, but young

Nina refused to play at her recital until her parents were placed in the front of the performance hall. This marked the beginning of Nina's strong voice and intolerance for unfairness toward Black people.

Nina was an incredibly talented pianist and she was accepted to study at the prestigious Juilliard School, with the plan that she'd then attend the Curtis Institute of Music in Philadelphia. Her family moved to Philadelphia knowing that she was talented enough to get in, but Nina, unfortunately, was denied a spot at the school. Hurt and disappointed, she took odd jobs and taught piano from her home for a short while.

Things began to look up when Nina landed a job performing at Midtown Bar and Grill in Atlantic City. She wasn't trained to be a singer, but the owner of the club told her she had to sing if she wanted to keep her job, so she did her best to sing like Billie Holiday and other starlets of the past. Until this time, Nina was known by her given name—Eunice Kathleen Waymon—but she changed her name to Nina Simone so her mother would not find out she was playing and singing non-church music.

To keep people's attention at the bar, Nina would spontaneously burst into playing classical music. This was when her name and style of music (a mixture of classical, soul, and jazz) was the root of who she would become as a music icon. One of the very few hit songs Nina released was "I Loves You, Porgy" in 1958.

In the 1960s, Nina released civil rights songs like "Old Jim Crow" and "Why? (The King of Love Is Dead)," which was about the killing of Dr. Martin Luther King Jr. Eventually Nina decided to leave the United States to live in other countries like Liberia and Barbados to escape racism and the silencing of her music by white record label executives who thought Nina was too radical. She finally settled in France, where she lived until her death. Nina was a strong-willed, unique, and complex musician who used her voice to cry out against injustice. Because Nina was passionate about everything she did, her songs were deeply emotional and haunting. Even her love songs had a tinge of sadness and heartbreak. Her fans connected with her intensity, as listening to her music makes one feel as if floating in a sea of beauty and pain.

Sister Nancy

(B. JANUARY 2, 1962)

DANCEHALL REGGAE

The First Lady of Dancehall

"I went to school, I could have done more,
but what I did was what I wanted—
and that was music."

—SISTER NANCY

Sister Nancy made history before her eighteenth birthday by becoming the first woman dancehall DJ in Jamaica. Dancehall is an upbeat form of reggae music in which mostly men would deejay records at parties, rhyming and entertaining the crowd while they danced.

Sister Nancy, whose real name is Ophlin Russell, grew up in a conservative Christian household in St. Andrew, Jamaica, with a large family. She had plenty of siblings to play with and learn from, but it was her older brother Robert, a well-known DJ in Kingston, Jamaica, who went by the name Brigadier Jerry, who inspired her to find what she truly loved in life. Sister Nancy loved music, and when she was a teenager, she began to go to dancehall parties, sometimes as the only girl in the entire crowd. At fifteen years old, with her brother's support, she became the first woman DJ on the dancehall scene, hopping on the mic and playing music for enthusiastic partygoers. She had fun and great success, and she toured often (she was also the first woman dancehall DJ to tour internationally).

In 1982, Sister Nancy released her first album, *One Two*, which had singles like "One Two" and "Transport Connection"—these songs spread like wildfire in Jamaica! But while it was true that Sister Nancy was doing well as a DJ, she wasn't making a lot of money doing what she loved. As time went on, she couldn't afford to live by just playing music, so she left that world and became an accountant.

In 1996, fourteen years after the release of her first album, Sister Nancy moved to America to continue her work in banking. Little did she know she'd find that her song "Bam Bam" was being sampled (which means bits and pieces of her song were used to make an entirely new song) by numerous hip-hop artists and was even featured in a Reebok commercial! Sister Nancy was very surprised because "Bam Bam" was not popular in Jamaica, but in America, hip-hop artists (the first being Main Source in 1991) were making her song a hit. "Bam Bam" was sampled more than seventy-three times by major artists including Jay-Z, Kanye West, and Alicia Keys. Because of this, Sister Nancy was able to actually receive money for the use of her song.

In 2016, Sister Nancy left her job as an accountant and went back to playing music— thirty years after she got her start. She is still making her dreams come true with the help of American hip-hop stars who were instrumental in helping her secure her rightful place in music history.

Skin

(B. AUGUST 3, 1967)

HARD ROCK

The Queen of British Hard Rock

"I refused to play the game."

—SKIN

Most people know the beautiful, haunting voice of artist Skin through her hard rock band, Skunk Anansie. Skin started the band with guitarist Ace, bass player Cass, and drummer Mark Richardson in 1994, and she quickly took the world by storm with her signature bald head and killer all-black outfits suited for a true rock star.

Skin (her birth name is Deborah Ann Dyer) grew up in Brixton, a district in London, England, with her Jamaican immigrant parents. At six years old she moved in with her grand-mother, who ran a nightclub in the basement of her house. This is where Skin learned about music and the nightclub scene, which prepared her for a lifelong career as a musician. She loved to listen to people's conversations, which gave her inspiration for writing songs, and she was also heavily influenced by the strong political climate in Brixton when she was growing up. When Skunk Anansie formed, the band focused their first album—1995's *Paranoid & Sunburnt*—on songs of protest, sharing their points of view on political topics as well as cultural and religious intolerance.

Skin's powerful soprano voice rang over loud, heavy hard-rock guitars and pounding drums, making her a rare Black woman rock star. She dominated in a musical realm made up of mostly male musicians. Skunk Anansie toured the world and became leaders of the Britpop and British rock music scene, but after seven years, in 2001, the group decided to break up.

However, this wasn't the end of Skin's career. In 2003, she released a solo album called *Fleshwounds* and then her next album, *Fake Chemical State*, came out in 2006. Three years later, Skunk Anansie decided to get back together. In total, the group has recorded six albums and sold more than four million records worldwide, making them one of the most successful British rock bands between the 1950s and the 2000s.

Skin—a tall, thin, mysterious-looking Black woman—is destined to go down in British rock history. She is wise and strong and loves herself for who she is. She never gave in to the pressures of the music industry to sing softer love songs and to dress in ultra-feminine clothing.

Skin is a role model to women and girls who feel different or live outside the box. She is a shining example that a woman can shave her head and still be beautiful. She can play with a heavy rock band and still emit grace and poise. She knows that her femininity is her own and can't be defined and ruled by what the world thinks she should be. These are the qualities that make her a rock and roll legend and a true inspiration to her generation as well as to girls of the future!

Bessie Smith

(APRIL 15, 1894, TO SEPTEMBER 26, 1937)

BLUES

The Empress of Blues

*"Listen to my story and
everything will come out true."*

—BESSIE SMITH

Bessie Smith was a strong, gregarious, and tough woman. It's no surprise, because she had to face a lot of troubles when she was young. Both of her parents passed away by the time she was ten years old, and she was raised by her older sister. To help make money for her family, Bessie sang on street corners.

As a young performer, Bessie auditioned for the Moses Stokes troupe and got a job dancing with Stokes's group of traveling performers—including the "Mother of the Blues," Ma Rainey. Rainey was impressed with Bessie's incredible talent and took her under her wing, teaching her and guiding her on how to be the best performer she could be. The group toured all over the American South and Bessie worked diligently to create a big enough fan base that by the time

she was twenty-four years old, she was able to start singing as a solo act. She moved to Atlanta, Georgia, to perform in theaters there.

Her live performances, showcasing her bellowing, unforgettable voice, were so good that Bessie was able to begin recording music, too. Her first single, "Down Hearted Blues," became a big hit and sold more than 700,000 copies. This was long before the Internet, so it was amazing that she was able to sell so many records on her first try. Just under a year later, Bessie had sold more than two million records!

Over the course of ten years, Bessie recorded more than 150 songs. But it wasn't just Bessie's recorded music that made her a big star. Not only was she a great singer, but she also was a songwriter, composing and singing her own songs like "Young Woman's Blues" and "You've Been a Good Ole Wagon."

Bessie Smith was powerful. Standing at six feet tall, with a curvy body and dark brown skin, she was in command of the room and the stage, and was known to be very straightforward. She could sometimes be quite mean to others, but people loved her for her brashness and strength.

During the 1920s, Bessie became the highest-paid Black singer and entertainer in America. She died tragically in a car crash when she was in her forties, but Bessie's music carries on, and the world knows and loves her as the true "Empress of Blues."

Ronnie Spector

(B. AUGUST 10, 1943)

ROCK AND ROLL

A Pioneer of Black Women in Rock

*"No one has their own identity
like the Ronettes did back in the day."*

—RONNIE SPECTOR

Ronnie Spector was a vivacious teenager with a unique background and a fashion style all her own. Her mother was Black and Native American and her father was Irish—this made Ronnie a groundbreaking figure for girls of color who hoped to participate in the world of rock and roll. She was a style icon with her hair teased sky high, her dramatic eye makeup, and her signature miniskirts. Ronnie was the "bad girl of rock and roll" because she and her group, the Ronettes, had an edgy look about them, which their fans loved!

Ronnie's story begins in Spanish Harlem, where she, her sister, and their cousin performed for their family on Saturday evenings. Ronnie loved the young Black pop stars Frankie Lymon and the Teenagers' style of bubble pop, along with their super-cool attitude. Their music

sparked a flame in Ronnie, inspiring her to form a group with four other girls in her family plus her cousin Ira, who was a boy. The group eventually performed at the world-famous Amateur Night at the Apollo Theater. For their performance, Ira was supposed to sing the lead vocals of Frankie Lymon and the Teenagers' hit "Why Do Fools Fall in Love," but when the music began, Ira froze. Ronnie decided to take the microphone and sing the lead part instead. After the show ended, some of the members of the group left, but her sister, Estelle, and her cousin Nedra would join Ronnie to become the iconic singing group the Ronettes.

One night in 1961, the girls stood outside the popular Peppermint Lounge nightclub, waiting to get inside. While they waited, the manager of the club saw them and thought they were dancers he had hired to perform behind the band that was playing that night. The girls went along with his story and got onstage, dancing the newest dance craze: the Twist! While they were dancing, Ronnie was handed the mic to sing. She did so well that the girls were offered a job dancing and performing at the club every night. This lucky break opened the door for the girls to sign a record deal with powerhouse producer Phil Spector.

Phil did an amazing job making music with the Ronettes, and their first album, *Presenting the Fabulous Ronettes Featuring Veronica*, has gone on to become one of the most important rock and roll albums of all time. The song "Be My Baby" was a major hit, and other songs like "(The Best Part of) Breakin' Up" and "Baby, I Love You" were also hugely popular in the 1960s. The Ronettes had become bona fide rock stars, but things changed after Ronnie married Phil Spector in 1968.

Ronnie's marriage to Phil was not good. He locked her in their big house for almost ten years and Ronnie wasn't allowed to leave because Phil was very controlling and didn't want her to meet new people or to sing anymore. Ronnie's music career went from a huge success to nothing at all. Eventually, she escaped from her house and broke out on her own again.

Ronnie revitalized her music career and recorded four albums: *Siren* (1980), *Unfinished Business* (1987), *The Last of the Rock Stars* (2006), and *English Heart* (2016). Ronnie is a survivor and has a heart of gold. Now in her seventies, she still performs onstage and doesn't have any plans to retire. Rock and roll is her life and her story is absolutely one for the ages.

Mavis Staples

(B. JULY 10, 1939)

R&B / GOSPEL

A Gospel Music Icon

*"I'm singing these songs to inspire you,
to keep you going, to lift you up and give you
a reason to get up in the morning."*

—MAVIS STAPLES

In 1950, long before Mavis Staples finished high school or recorded her first solo album, she was a singer in her family's gospel group, the Staple Singers, which included her father, Roebuck "Pops" Staples; her sisters, Cleotha and Yvonne; and her brother, Pervis. The group traveled and sang in local churches around Chicago and released their first hit song, "Uncloudy Day," in 1956.

Mavis and her family would go on to be spiritual leaders of the civil rights movement after recording a song called "Why? (Am I Treated So Bad)" in 1957. The song was about the Little Rock Nine, the first group of Black students who attended

a mostly white school in Arkansas after segregation became illegal. This song led Dr. Martin Luther King Jr. to ask the Staple Singers to perform at many of his speaking engagements, as their mixture of music and activism brought hope and strength to the cause (one such example was their song "Long Walk to D.C.," highlighting the years of protests that were taking place). The Staple Singers climbed to their musical peak in the 1970s with the release of their well-known song "I'll Take You There."

Mavis loved her family very much, but it was important for her to find her own voice and strike out on her own. She released her first solo album, *Mavis Staples*, in 1969, and *Only for the Lonely* in 1970. Then, in 1984, Mavis became friends with the music superstar Prince. They recorded three albums together: *Mavis Staples* in 1984, *Time Waits for No One* in 1989, and *The Voice* in 1993. These albums showed that Mavis was good at working with younger musicians. Her music was sampled by hip-hop artists Salt-N-Pepa, Ludacris, and others. She had a good connection with young songwriters that made her music feel fresh even though she had been singing for more than fifty years!

In 1996, she released a collaboration with musician Lucky Peterson called *Spirituals & Gospel: Dedicated to Mahalia Jackson*—an album that paid respect to the iconic gospel singer, who was a family friend and a musical inspiration to Mavis. She also had a close friendship with famous folk singer Bob Dylan. In fact, Dylan fell in love with Mavis and asked for her hand in marriage when they were young! She didn't marry him, but they did record "Gonna Change My Way of Thinking" in 2003 and toured together in 2016. Mavis released her most recent album, *We Get By*, in 2019 just before her eightieth birthday!

Mavis has a laugh that brightens any room she enters. She's young at heart and lives life to the very fullest. Her gospel music has been able to touch diverse audiences because of her willingness to experiment with different producers, which makes her albums feel fresh and youthful. Her music is down-to-earth and simply lovely to listen to. Her lifetime of musical excellence will guide future gospel musicians to create authentic, touching music.

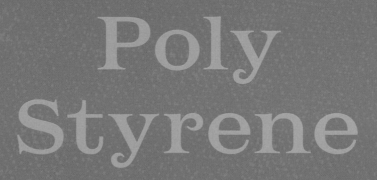

Poly Styrene

(JULY 3, 1957, TO APRIL 25, 2011)

PUNK

The Pioneer of Women in Punk

"Some people think little girls should be seen and not heard. But I think, 'OH BONDAGE UP YOURS!'"

—POLY STYRENE

Poly Styrene had a style all her own. She was an explorer from an early age. Poly wasn't very interested in school, even though her mother, who raised her as a single parent, thought teaching her to type would help her finish her education and find a professional career. On the contrary, when Poly was fifteen, she packed her bags and hitchhiked around Europe, going to music festivals and living in hippie culture, which was very exciting to her. While she was young, Poly tried different life paths, giving fashion design and pop-reggae singing a chance. When she was eighteen, she recorded her first song using her real name, Marianne Joan Elliott-Said, but she didn't feel that singing reggae was ultimately a good fit for her.

Everything changed for Poly in 1976, when she attended a Sex Pistols concert and discovered her love of punk music. Soon after the show, she saw an ad in the local newspaper looking for "Young punx who want to stick it together." Because of her love of community and what she saw at this punk show, Poly decided to start her own punk rock band. When she looked for a name to call her band, she knew she wanted something that described the times she was living in, so she chose her band name, which she felt was synthetic and not authentic: X-Ray Spex.

Her band included guitar player Jak Airport, bass player Paul Dean, drummer Paul "B.P." Hurding, and saxophonist Lora Logic. They released their first song, "Oh Bondage Up Yours!," in 1977, and later put out a full album called *Germfree Adolescents*. This album is now considered a classic punk record and Poly Styrene is said to be a woman who sparked the American female punk scene known as riot grrrl, where women sang heavy punk songs pushing back against violence and stereotypes of all women.

Poly was a natural onstage, wearing metal braces on her teeth and cool military-style jackets and hats. She was strong, confident, and wonderful to watch while performing.

X-Ray Spex broke up after recording their first and only album, but Poly went on to record solo albums entitled *Translucence* in 1980, *Gods & Goddesses* in 1986, and *Flower Aeroplane* in 2004. Her music touched people all over the world for many years, and she performed at music festivals right up to the time of her death in 2011. Poly's daughter, Celeste Bell, made a documentary called *Poly Styrene: I Am a Cliché* to share the memory of her mother and her impact on women punk musicians. Poly was unique and will never lose her place as an important person who changed punk music forever.

Sister Rosetta Tharpe

(MARCH 20, 1915, TO OCTOBER 9, 1973)

ROCK AND ROLL

The Godmother of Rock and Roll

*"Can't no man play like me.
I play better than a man."*

—SISTER ROSETTA THARPE

Legend has it that Sister Rosetta Tharpe influenced the sound of modern rock and roll. She was the first to make the electric guitar popular in gospel and soul music, creating a new sound that inspired rock stars like the Rolling Stones, Elvis Presley, and Little Richard.

She was born Rosetta Nubin to a talented musician mother who played the mandolin and worked as a traveling preacher. Her mother encouraged little Rosetta to play guitar so she

could use her instrument to spread the gospel. By the time she was six, Rosetta and her mom had set out on the road accompanying a troupe of musicians and ministers to share their music with others. A few years later, in the mid-1920s, Rosetta and her mother moved to Chicago, where Rosetta became known as a prodigy (meaning a young musical genius). No one had seen such a young Black girl play the guitar so well.

At nineteen years old, Rosetta married a preacher named Thomas Tharpe, and she changed her last name to his. Their marriage lasted only four years, but Sister Rosetta Tharpe kept her married name until the end of her life.

At twenty-three, Rosetta and her mother moved to New York, which helped Rosetta's music career blossom quickly. One of the first songs she recorded was "Rock Me," a song she is still famous for today. "Rock Me" has joyful gospel lyrics, and Rosetta's upbeat guitar is what became the sound of early rock and roll. Every song Sister Rosetta Tharpe released in her first years of recording albums became a hit. In 1938, she played famous nightclubs and concert halls like the Cotton Club and Carnegie Hall, touching new audiences who instantly loved her unique gospel style.

As Sister Rosetta became more and more famous with jazz and blues music fans, the more American Christian and gospel communities got upset that she was playing in nightclubs to people they considered to be ungodly. Even though Sister Rosetta made it a point to play mostly gospel songs because that was the music she grew up with and loved very much, she felt she had a bigger purpose in her life—to touch people all over the world with all types of music.

Sister Rosetta toured for many years, and her most famous shows occurred in Europe in 1964, where she performed many of her hit songs, such as "Up Above My Head" and "Strange Things Happening Every Day." Her UK shows are said to have sparked the creation of early British rock and roll.

Without Sister Rosetta's music and world travels, it's hard to know what music would sound like today. She is the "Godmother of Rock and Roll," laying the groundwork for modern music

Big Mama Thornton

(DECEMBER 11, 1926, TO JULY 25, 1984)

BLUES

A Blues Music Groundbreaker

"White or black. Rich or poor. If you ever had your heart broken you have the right to sing the blues."

—BIG MAMA THORNTON

Willie Mae "Big Mama" Thornton learned about music from an early age while growing up as a member of a church in Alabama. Her father was a minister and her mother a singer. Her mother died when Willie Mae was a little girl, and so Willie Mae had to quit school and get a job working in a local tavern to help the family make ends meet.

In 1940, when she was just fourteen, Willie Mae's singing talent was discovered by the blues and gospel vocalist Diamond Teeth Mary and she soon began to travel as a singer with Sammy Green's Hot Harlem Revue. Willie Mae was inspired by popular singers of her time, including Bessie Smith and Memphis Minnie, and it showed through her vocal style and performances.

She was called "Big Mama" by fellow blues musicians because of her strong, curvy body and self-confidence.

A few years later, Big Mama signed with a record label and recorded one of her most popular songs, "Hound Dog." This song was later made famous by the rock and roll titan Elvis Presley, but Big Mama was the first to sing it. She was a commanding and creative singer, bringing attitude and a confident sound to every song she sang. Even though Elvis made this particular song a huge hit, the song was actually about a Black woman not accepting the dishonest behavior of men.

In 1965, Big Mama found success in Europe while traveling as a singer with the American Folk Blues Festival. She soon recorded her first full album, *Big Mama Thornton—In Europe*, followed by 1966's *Big Mama Thornton with the Muddy Waters Blues Band*, where she played with the influential blues guitarist Muddy Waters. She loved the blues but she also thought it was incredibly important to record a gospel album because of her roots in the church. She was able to make this wish happen by recording the lovely gospel album *Saved* in 1973.

Big Mama Thornton toured and recorded albums throughout the 1970s and '80s, up until she passed away. Her deep voice, positive energy, and love for music allowed her to have a lengthy career and to perform for her entire life. She was brave, creative, and very passionate about music, and there is no doubt that Big Mama Thornton had a hand in shaping the blues music we hear today.

Tina Turner

(B. NOVEMBER 26, 1939)

R&B / ROCK AND ROLL

The Queen of Rock and Roll

*"Physical strength in a woman—
that's what I am."*

—TINA TURNER

Selling more than 100 million records worldwide, Tina Turner is one of the most accomplished American musicians of all time.

She was born a poor sharecropper's daughter in Nutbush, Tennessee, and learned to sing in church. As a little girl, Tina (whose given name is Anna Mae Bullock) learned to pick cotton, and she worked as a housekeeper once she became a teenager.

Tina's music career began when she found herself mesmerized by a performance of Ike Turner's Kings of Rhythm at the Manhattan Club in East St. Louis, Illinois. One fateful night in 1957, Tina decided to grab the microphone from the Kings of Rhythm's drummer and sing a version of blues musician B.B. King's "You Know I Love You." Her performance

got the attention of the band's leader, Ike Turner, who asked Tina to be a regular singer with the Kings of Rhythm. By 1958, Tina was in the recording studio working on a song called "Boxtop" (at that time, she was performing under the name Little Ann). She began to tour with Ike and worked as a songwriter and backup vocalist for studio recordings. While Tina's career was budding, she also began to fall in love with Ike.

Tina eventually married Ike, and throughout the 1960s Ike and Tina Turner would become one of the most electrifying rock and roll groups in the world, wowing audiences with signature songs such as "Proud Mary," "Nutbush City Limits," and "River Deep—Mountain High." The pair toured with the popular English rock band the Rolling Stones in the UK in 1966 and then in the United States in 1969. They performed regularly on popular TV programs like *The Ed Sullivan Show*, which helped them become incredibly famous with American audiences.

Tina had a powerful, raspy voice, and her quick, gyrating dance moves—along with her backup singers, the Ikettes—made her a memorable, exciting performer to watch. No one could deny her star power, but due to the stormy relationship between Tina and Ike, the band broke up in the mid-1970s.

Tina worked very hard as a solo act throughout the late 1970s and early '80s, touring and performing in clubs around America and Europe, but she wasn't able to land another hit record during that time. This didn't keep her from giving her music and live shows all she had. And her determination paid off, because in 1983, her version of soul singer Al Green's "Let's Stay Together" became a surprise hit and marked the beginning of Tina's return to stardom.

Tina's 1984 album, *Private Dancer*, sold more than twelve million copies globally, and her iconic hit "What's Love Got to Do with It" was a number one top-selling song. Two other singles, "Better Be Good to Me" and "Private Dancer," also sold well, and in 1985, Tina ventured out on her first world tour as a solo artist.

Tina recorded five more albums, released three books, acted in several movies, and became the subject of a Broadway show written about her life, *Tina: The Tina Turner Musical*. In 2020, she worked on a remix of "What's Love Got to Do with It" with Norwegian artist Kygo. Tina has had a hit song every decade for the past seventy years in the United Kingdom. Her book, *Happiness Becomes You: A Guide to Changing Your Life for Good*, was published in 2020. Tina currently lives in Switzerland and is a global icon whose fire will never dim.

Ari Up

(JANUARY 17, 1962, TO OCTOBER 20, 2010)

PUNK / REGGAE

Punk Rock Royalty

"I'm a rock 'n' roll baby. I was one of the last actually born into rock, in the middle of it."

—ARI UP

Ari Up is one of the most unique women in music history. She was born in a time when punk rock had emerged as an amazing force in the British music scene. Her father was a German musician and her mother, Nora Forster, was well connected in the music industry. (In fact, Nora knew iconic musicians like Jimi Hendrix!) Ariane Daniela Forster grew up around a blossoming punk rock music community, and her exposure to the music grew even more when her mother married Sid Vicious, a member of the prolific punk band the Sex Pistols. Ari's home was often full of artists, music makers, and all-around interesting people.

The lead member of the punk band the Clash, Joe Strummer, was Ari's guitar teacher. Once she learned how to play and sing, there was no holding Ari back. She grew up in Germany, and even though English was not her first language, she learned to speak it well enough to sing in English. In 1976, fourteen-year-old Ari started her very own band called the Slits.

The original members of the Slits were drummer Paloma McLardy—also known as Palmolive—bassist Suzy Gutsy, and guitarist Kate Korus. The Slits' music was a fun mix of reggae and punk rock, and just a few years later, the band went on the road to tour with the Clash and were even featured performers in a film called *The Punk Rock Movie*.

In 1979, the Slits released their first full-length album, *Cut*, which included an amazing girl-power anthem called "Typical Girls," championing the awesomeness of being different and the boringness of being like everyone else. The Slits were a band that opened doors to the riot grrrl punk scene as well as all-women bands like Bikini Kill, Bratmobile, and Sleater-Kinney.

In 1981, the Slits broke up, and Ari went on to have three children, moving all over the world to places like Indonesia, Belize, and Jamaica. Over the years she continued to play music both with a band called the New Age Steppers and also as a solo musician. In 2005, after more than twenty years, the Slits reunited, and they released *Revenge of the Killer Slits* in 2006. They toured the United States, Australia, and Japan in 2007. The Slits released an album called *Trapped Animal* in 2009 and continued to perform as much as they could.

Sadly, the Slits reunion was cut short when Ari Up died in 2010 at the young age of forty-eight. The band's last song, "Lazy Slam," was released after she died per Ari's request before she passed away. She was a huge influence in the world of all-female punk rock bands. The riot grrrl music movement would arguably not exist without Ari's music, free spirit, and unique punk attitude. She was a true trailblazer and punk rock icon.

Sarah Vaughan

(MARCH 27, 1924, TO APRIL 3, 1990)

JAZZ

The Divine One

"It sure is a nice feeling to know that people will remember you after you're gone, that you'll manage to be a little bit of history."

—SARAH VAUGHAN

Jazz singer Sarah Vaughan was commonly known as "Sassy" because of her sense of humor and delightful approach to singing. She often giggled and laughed while onstage, giving her performance a sense of playful entertainment.

As a little girl, Sarah grew up in a churchgoing family and had a musical background. Her father played piano and guitar and her mother sang during church services. Sarah began learning to play piano at seven years old and then the organ at twelve. She also took after her mother by singing in the church's choir while playing the organ.

By the time she was a teenager, Sarah was sneaking into nightclubs to both listen to the music and be a part of the social scene. She had a dream of becoming a nightclub singer, and

she found a job performing at the Piccadilly Club in Newark, New Jersey, in the late 1930s. By 1942, she was so good at performing that her best friend insisted that she sing at the Apollo in New York City during its Amateur Night. Sarah went and won the competition! One of the prizes was that she would be able to sing at the Apollo for one week, and during that week, she got a chance to open for one of the most powerful singers of the time: Ella Fitzgerald.

In 1943, Sarah performed with jazz pianist Earl Hines's Band, whose members included jazz icons Charlie Parker and Dizzy Gillespie. In 1944, Sarah recorded her first song, "I'll Wait and Pray," with a newer big band led by her friend Billy Eckstine. Sarah sang so beautifully that she was asked to record as a solo singer. By 1945, Sarah was well on her way to becoming a world-class star. She recorded many songs in a short period, including "Time and Again," "Lover Man," "Don't Blame Me," "Everything I Have Is Yours," and "Body and Soul." She also scored her first hit songs with "Tenderly" (1947) and "It's Magic" (1948).

In 1949, Sarah was also the star of her own radio show called *Songs by Sarah Vaughan*, where she sang jazz songs with a small band. The show played five days a week and was recorded at the Clique Club in New York City.

Sarah continued to have success through 1953, when she signed with the major jazz record label Columbia Records. There, she ended up singing more pop than jazz songs. Her voice was creamy and sweet to the ears. One of her best-selling songs at Columbia was "Broken Hearted Melody," and she had continued success in the 1960s and '70s. Her 1971 album, *A Time in My Life*, showed her ability to connect with younger listeners by playing the songs of John Lennon. Sarah later recorded her signature song, "Send in the Clowns" from the musical *A Little Night Music*. She also had success later in her career, winning an Emmy Award for her symphony performance with the New Jersey Symphony that was aired on PBS in 1980. She continued to perform and win awards throughout the '80s. Her final album *Brazilian Romance* was recorded in 1987. She died in 1990.

Sarah traveled all over the world recording live albums in countries like Denmark, Japan, and Brazil, and she played with lavish orchestras. She was sophisticated and classy, and her bubbly humor made others adore her. Her silky vocals made her love ballads stunning, and her fans could not resist the loving embrace of her songs. Her legacy as a jazz singer will truly last for generations.

Dionne Warwick

(B. DECEMBER 12, 1940)

R&B / POP

A Major R&B Hitmaker

*"I don't think there's anything I can't do.
I have no regrets."*

—DIONNE WARWICK

Beloved 1960s R&B pop singer Dionne Warwick came from a family of singers. During her childhood, many members of Dionne's family, including her aunt Cissy Houston (mother of the world-famous 1980s and '90s pop singer Whitney Houston), sang in a group called the Drinkard Singers. Her musical upbringing moved six-year-old Dionne to sing in the church where her grandfather ministered. By age seven she was able to read music and play piano, and she soon became a richly talented gospel singer.

When she was a teenager, Dionne and her sister Dee Dee started a gospel group called the Gospelaires, which gave her even more training to become the amazing singer she is today. Dionne studied piano and music education while in college and sang backup for artists like

Dinah Washington in recording studios in New York City. Her voice was so beautiful that it shone through even while she sang backup. Two songwriters—Hal David and Burt Bacharach—eventually heard her vocals and decided to write songs for her.

In 1962, Dionne's first song, "Don't Make Me Over," became extremely popular and sparked the beginning of her successful solo career. Her biggest hit song by far is "I Say a Little Prayer," and she is also well-known for "Do You Know the Way to San Jose" and the 1964 hit "Walk On By." Dionne also sang the theme song for the 1968 movie *Valley of the Dolls*, which brought her wonderful success.

Dionne has a silky, elegant voice that can never be mistaken for anyone else's. Her big smile and dreamy presence make her a dynamic and mesmerizing singer to watch on television and onstage. During the 1970s she had some success with her beautiful solo music, but in the 1980s, she began to make songs with other top artists. She recorded the song "That's What Friends Are For" with Gladys Knight, Elton John, and Stevie Wonder, as well as "We Are the World" with Tina Turner, Michael Jackson, Diana Ross, and many others. Both songs were recorded and performed for charity to help people all over the world, and they boosted Dionne's career even further.

Now in her eighties, Dionne Warwick continues to perform her music all over the world. Many of her fans have loved her for more than fifty years, and it's crystal clear that she loves them back! She was a Goodwill Ambassador for the Food and Agriculture Organization of the United Nations, which helps people around the world to have access to food and clean water. As recently as 2020, she hosted a virtual National COVID-19 Remembrance for those who lost their lives in the battle with the virus. She very much cares about her fans and people who have suffered in their lives, and gives back through her generous deeds and her beautiful music.

Dinah Washington

(AUGUST 29, 1924, TO DECEMBER 14, 1963)

JAZZ

The Queen of the Jukeboxes

*"I can sing anything,
anything at all."*

—DINAH WASHINGTON

In the 1930s, while Dinah Washington was a little girl and still in elementary school, she played piano and sang with her church choir. Her mother was a music teacher and was instrumental in giving Dinah (who was born Ruth Lee Jones) the confidence to take any opportunity to sing and perform in the church. By the time she was a teenager, Dinah advanced to directing a choir and was soon asked to join a gospel group, the Sallie Martin Gospel Singers.

Dinah decided, however, to play music outside of the church and left high school to perform in clubs around Chicago. It was at the Garrick Stage Bar that she would be heard by the club's owner and hired as his establishment's official singer. It is said that Dinah played the upstairs stage while Billie Holiday performed downstairs.

With a steady singing job and a dynamic new name—said to be given to her by talent manager Joe Glazer—Dinah attracted the attention of bandleader Lionel Hampton, who invited her to sing with his band. Soon after joining Hampton's group, she recorded her very first song, "Evil Gal Blues," which became a hit.

After this, Dinah's life and career became a whirlwind of fame, fortune, and, sometimes, a lot of trouble. Dinah was known to have a moody temper, but she worked very hard and people loved her very much. She recorded more than four hundred songs between 1946 and 1961. She is most famous for her version of the beautiful song "What a Diff'rence a Day Makes," which was the biggest hit of her career, as well as "Unforgettable," where Dinah sings with a loving and longing voice in a rich tone.

Dinah could sing *anything*. In fact, she performed country, pop, jazz, and blues. This allowed her to touch fans who liked many kinds of music. She became one of the richest and most successful women artists of her time and was known to be generous and caring to her family throughout her life.

Sadly, Dinah died in 1963 at the very young age of thirty-nine years old. Even though she had a short life, Dinah continues to be a shining light in the world of music, and her legacy will certainly never be forgotten.

Nancy Wilson

(FEBRUARY 20, 1937, TO DECEMBER 13, 2018)

JAZZ / POP

A Powerful Voice in Jazz

*"I wanted to do the music,
but not at the expense of being happy."*

—NANCY WILSON

Growing up in Chillicothe, Ohio, Nancy Wilson knew she was going to make music by the time she was four years old, she was deeply aware that she was destined to become a singer. She put her heart into her singing, and by the time she was ten, Nancy was a lead soloist in her church's choir. At fifteen, she won a talent contest that offered her the chance to appear two times a week on a TV show called *Skyline Melodies*. She performed so well on the program that she ended up becoming the host! But Nancy was just beginning to rise as a star. She took another leap in her early music career by singing and traveling with the Rusty Bryant Carolyn Club Big Band, touring Canada and America's Midwest.

In 1959, at the suggestion of a friend, jazz saxophonist Julian "Cannonball" Adderley,

Nancy moved to New York City with the hope of signing a record deal with Capitol Records. She quickly got a day job working as a secretary and sang in nightclubs after work. She later attracted a lucky opportunity to sing as a fill-in at a popular nightclub called the Blue Morocco. Her voice was so beautiful and poised that Nancy was asked to sing at the nightclub four nights a week. Within one month, she had signed with Capitol Records, making her dream come true.

In 1962, Nancy recorded a jazz album with her friend Cannonball Adderley titled *Nancy Wilson/Cannonball Adderley*. This album followed her first hit song, "Guess Who I Saw Today," and between 1960 and 1962, Nancy released five albums. The biggest hit of her career was the dreamy R&B song "(You Don't Know) How Glad I Am," which she released in 1964.

Following all of her recording success, in 1967 Nancy scored her own NBC TV show called *The Nancy Wilson Show*. She had to work hard to balance her music and her TV career as she appeared on dozens of shows between the 1960s and '90s.

Nancy's voice and musical style were sophisticated and classy. She made every song she sang sound like a beautiful lullaby. Her charm and grace brought her many opportunities in life. And even though she wasn't a trained singer, Nancy's gift was that she was hardworking. Throughout her fifty-year career, she recorded more than fifty studio albums. She was also an important civil rights advocate, like many other Black women musicians of her era. Nancy lived a full life and was an active singer and actress until the 2010s. She died in 2018, leaving a huge and impressive collection of music for the world to continue to enjoy.

GLOSSARY
OF MUSIC TERMS

ALBUM: a collection of songs put together and published on a record, tape, disc, or online grouping and sold as a single unit

ARRANGER: a person who adapts or alters an existing piece of music for different voices and/or instruments

BACKUP SINGER/VOCALIST: a person who sings secondary to, or behind, the lead or main singer on a song or album

BIG BAND: usually a larger grouping of musicians and/or singers that play jazz or swing music

COMPOSER: a person who writes music

DJ: an abbreviation for "disc jockey," which is a person who plays recorded music for a party, dance club, or another large event

GENRE: a category of music that showcases a certain form, content, or style. Musical genres covered in this book include blues, classical, dancehall, folk, funk, gospel, hip-hop, jazz, neo-soul, pop, punk, reggae, R&B, rock and roll, soul, and world music.

IMPROVISATION: a way to play music in which a singer, solo instrumentalist, or group of musicians sings or plays new music on the spot without any written composition

LEAD SINGER: the head or key person singing in a group musical ensemble

LYRICS: the words to a particular song

PRIMA DONNA: the main female singer, usually in an operatic or concert hall setting

RECORD LABEL: a company that gives contracts to singers and/or musical groups to record songs and albums and often controls the rights to those recordings

SCAT: a type of jazz singing that involves the singer making nonsense words or sounds to a melody

SOLOIST: a person who sings a song by herself or who performs a piece of music with only one vocal part

SONGSTRESS: a woman singer

SONGWRITER: someone who composes or writes words or music for songs, usually songs that are performed by popular or rock singers or groups

VOCALIST: a singer (usually a professional)

INDEX

SADE ADU • ERYKAH BADU • ANITA BAKER • BEYONCÉ • DEE DEE BRIDGEWATER • BETTY CARTER • TRACY C

HOLIDAY • LENA HORNE • JANET JACKSON • MAHALIA JACKSON • ETTA JAMES • CHAKA KHAN • ANGÉLIQUE K

• MEMPHIS MINNIE • ODETTA • THE POINTER SISTERS • LEONTYNE PRICE • QUEEN LATIFAH • MA RAINEY • MIN

• MAVIS STAPLES • POLY STYRENE • SISTER ROSETTA THARPE • BIG MAMA THORNTON • TINA TURNER • ARI

ANITA BAKER • BEYONCÉ • DEE DEE BRIDGEWATER • BETTY CARTER • TRACY CHAPMAN • NATALIE COLE • ELI

JACKSON • MAHALIA JACKSON • ETTA JAMES • CHAKA KHAN • ANGÉLIQUE KIDJO • GLADYS KNIGHT • PATTI

• THE POINTER SISTERS • LEONTYNE PRICE • QUEEN LATIFAH • MA RAINEY • MINNIE RIPERTON • DIANA RO

STYRENE • SISTER ROSETTA THARPE • BIG MAMA THORNTON • TINA TURNER • ARI UP • SARAH VAUGHAN •

• DEE DEE BRIDGEWATER • BETTY CARTER • TRACY CHAPMAN • NATALIE COLE • ELIZABETH COTTEN • ELLA

JACKSON • ETTA JAMES • CHAKA KHAN • ANGÉLIQUE KIDJO • GLADYS KNIGHT • PATTI LABELLE • ABBEY LINC

• LEONTYNE PRICE • QUEEN LATIFAH • MA RAINEY • MINNIE RIPERTON • DIANA ROSS • JILL SCOTT • NINA SIM

THARPE • BIG MAMA THORNTON • TINA TURNER • ARI UP • SARAH VAUGHAN • DIONNE WARWICK • DINAH

• BETTY CARTER • TRACY CHAPMAN • NATALIE COLE • ELIZABETH COTTEN • ELLA FITZGERALD • ROBERTA F

CHAKA KHAN • ANGÉLIQUE KIDJO • GLADYS KNIGHT • PATTI LABELLE • ABBEY LINCOLN • DARLENE LOVE •

QUEEN LATIFAH • MA RAINEY • MINNIE RIPERTON • DIANA ROSS • JILL SCOTT • NINA SIMONE • SISTER NANC

THORNTON • TINA TURNER • ARI UP • SARAH VAUGHAN • DIONNE WARWICK • DINAH WASHINGTON • NANC

CHAPMAN • NATALIE COLE • ELIZABETH COTTEN • ELLA FITZGERALD • ROBERTA FLACK • ARETHA FRANKLIN

KIDJO • GLADYS KNIGHT • PATTI LABELLE • ABBEY LINCOLN • DARLENE LOVE • BARBARA LYNN • RITA MARL

• MINNIE RIPERTON • DIANA ROSS • JILL SCOTT • NINA SIMONE • SISTER NANCY • SKIN • BESSIE SMITH • RO

• ARI UP • SARAH VAUGHAN • DIONNE WARWICK • DINAH WASHINGTON • NANCY WILSON • SADE ADU • ERY

• ELIZABETH COTTEN • ELLA FITZGERALD • ROBERTA FLACK • ARETHA FRANKLIN • BILLIE HOLIDAY • LENA H

PATTI LABELLE • ABBEY LINCOLN • DARLENE LOVE • BARBARA LYNN • RITA MARLEY • MC LYTE • MEMPHIS MIN

ROSS • JILL SCOTT • NINA SIMONE • SISTER NANCY • SKIN • BESSIE SMITH • RONNIE SPECTOR • MAVIS STAP

• DIONNE WARWICK • DINAH WASHINGTON • NANCY WILSON • SADE ADU • ERYKAH BADU • ANITA BAKER •

FITZGERALD • ROBERTA FLACK • ARETHA FRANKLIN • BILLIE HOLIDAY • LENA HORNE • JANET JACKSON • MAH

• DARLENE LOVE • BARBARA LYNN • RITA MARLEY • MC LYTE • MEMPHIS MINNIE • ODETTA • THE POINTER

SIMONE • SISTER NANCY • SKIN • BESSIE SMITH • RONNIE SPECTOR • MAVIS STAPLES • POLY STYRENE • SISTE

WASHINGTON • NANCY WILSON • SADE ADU • ERYKAH BADU • ANITA BAKER • BEYONCÉ • DEE DEE BRIDGEW

• ARETHA FRANKLIN • BILLIE HOLIDAY • LENA HORNE • JANET JACKSON • MAHALIA JACKSON • ETTA JAMES

LYNN • RITA MARLEY • MC LYTE • MEMPHIS MINNIE • ODETTA • THE POINTER SISTERS • LEONTYNE PRICE • (

BESSIE SMITH • RONNIE SPECTOR • MAVIS STAPLES • POLY STYRENE • SISTER ROSETTA THARPE • BIG MAMA